6.95

LET THE EARTH REJOICE!

LET THE EARTH REJOICE!

A Biblical Theology of Holistic Mission

William A. Dyrness

CROSSWAY BOOKS • WESTCHESTER, ILLINOIS
A DIVISION OF GOOD NEWS PUBLISHERS

To my wife,
Grace Roberts Dyrness,
whose life praises God

Scripture quotations are taken from the *Revised Standard Version* unless otherwise indicated.

Let the Earth Rejoice! Copyright © 1983 by William A. Dyrness. Published by Crossway Books, a division of Good News Publishers, Westchester, Illinois 60153.

Cover photo: Jim Whitmer
First printing, 1983.

Library of Congress Catalog Card Number 83-70322
ISBN 0-89107-282-9

Contents

LET THE EARTH REJOICE!

Preface

This book sets out to inquire whether there is a biblical warrant for seeing a political and social dimension to our missions and evangelism. It makes no pretense of being a complete biblical theology of mission though it may make a modest contribution in that direction. On the other hand it does not seek to provide any practical help as to how evangelism should be carried out when confronted with the complex questions of poverty and economic disparities that exist today. It seeks rather to point out a dimension of the biblical account that is often overlooked and that has great implications for Christians seeking to give a witness to Christ in the 1980s. The book had its impetus when World Vision Asia approached the Institute of Studies for Asian Church Culture (ISACC) in Manila to ask them to do a biblical study and multimedia set that would help their workers understand the work of development in a biblical framework. From this assignment grew a course that I taught at the Asian Theological Seminary on a Biblical Theology of Holistic Mission. As the study proceeded, however, it became more and more apparent that the application of these insights was much wider than those working in development and included not only missionaries and evangelists working cross-culturally but Americans seeking to wrestle with the political and social dimensions of their faith.

As everything carried out in Asia this project received a

good deal of community encouragement and support. I am
very grateful to Mac Bradshaw of World Vision Asia for his
creative stimulus in this and many other projects; to Ruth
Castillo for her patient and competent typing; and to Marlon
Roldan and Melba Maggay, ISACC leaders, who gave me
great freedom and encouragement to pursue my writing. I
am also grateful to Peter Davids, dear colleague and friend
at New College, who kindly read the manuscript and patiently made valuable comments on it. These stand for many
others from whom I have learned and whose fellowship in
the gospel is my most treasured possession.

William Dyrness
New College Berkeley
March 1983

Introduction

Context of the Discussion

It is safe to say that the most urgent questions in mission discussions of the last decade have centered on the role of the Church in the midst of complex social and economic problems. Questions about the relation between evangelism and social concern have become particularly urgent in Third World situations where an overwhelming majority of the population is poor. Theological movements such as liberation theology in Latin America began to reread Scripture in the light of a people struggling with poverty and exploitation and to ask: what does the Good News mean in such a situation?

Gustavo Gutierrez, a Catholic theologian, brought these issues to the attention of the thological world with his book *A Theology of Liberation*. He complained that theology as it has traditionally been conceived does not confront the issues faced by Latin Americans. In fact, the machinations of rich nations in general—all their economic strategies, even their developmental and relief organizations—have contributed to the continued dependence and exploitation that characterizes relations between first and third worlds. Things are not getting better; they are growing worse. As a result, he believes an entirely new approach is called for in which "liberation" rather than "conversion" or "development" becomes the goal of Christian mission. He points out that:

> Liberation expresses the aspiration of oppressed peoples and social classes (and) at a deeper level . . . can be applied to an understanding of history. . . . In the Bible, Christ is presented as the one who brings us liberation. Christ the Savior liberates man from sin, which is the ultimate root of all disruption of friendship and of all injustice and oppression. Christ makes men truly free, that is to say, he enables man to live in communion with him; and this is the basis for all human brotherhood.[1]

Evangelism and mission conceived in these terms, he believes, will highlight the relevance of Christ's work for the struggle for human justice and dignity throughout history.

Such attempts to define mission in broader terms have had a wide influence on both Catholic and Protestant theologians. Commenting on a recent Conference on Mission and Evangelism of the World Council of Churches, Commission director Emilio Castro said:

> If we take seriously the fact that the proclamation of the gospel of the Kingdom is above all for the poor, we are faced with a clear calling to our world missionary commitment, and within that same commitment, an engagement towards justice, in order to announce the Gospel that really is Good News to the downtrodden of the earth.[2]

This means that Christians will often proclaim Christ from within the search for solutions to the human problems they face today.

Many evangelicals, however, have taken exception to this broader view of mission, feeling that placing emphasis on social concerns threatens the centrality of the biblical message. Peter Beyerhaus, a German missiologist, complained some time ago that:

> At least since the preparation for the Uppsala Assembly in 1968, not Christianization and Church planting, but humani-

zation and radical change of social structures seem to be the
new ecumenical missionary strategy.[3]

He believes this displaces the Church's primary task, which
is to preach the gospel and encourage Church growth.
Humanizing effects, of course, are an indirect effect of the
ministry—an "anticipatory reflection of the coming kingdom."[4] But incorporation into the body of Christ must remain the Church's primary goal. Professor Arthur Johnston
of Trinity Seminary insists similarly that "historically the
mission of the Church is evangelism alone."[5] The broadening of the scope of the Church's mission, he believes, betrays Christ's command in Matthew 28 and shows the influence of another gospel.

   These are important discussions and while it is not
possible for us to pursue them here, the interested reader
may consult the literature that lays out these issues.[6] What is
clear, however, is that Christians seeking to understand
their faith in the context of the Third World, even if they
may be disposed to agree theologically with Messrs. Beyerhaus and Johnston, cannot be content to dismiss the challenge of liberation theology so easily. For in many parts of
the world the great present fact is a consuming thirst for
progress and development; ambitious government and private programs seek to better the lot of the ⅔ to ¾ of the
population which is poor. Christians living amidst such oppression and underdevelopment are naturally moved to ask
what biblical grounds there might be for the process of development (and of liberation) which people around them so
earnestly hope for. Is there any relation between the Christian hope and these human hopes and aspirations? Does the
wish for a better life have no relation to the salvation God
offers to all people?

   There have been attempts by evangelicals to deal specifically with the questions of poverty and development. Most
notable among these is Ronald Sider's *Rich Christians in an
Age of Hunger*.[7] This has been followed by several attempts
(by Hancock, Sider and others) to develop a theology of
development.[8] These have all made a valuable contribution,

and without their stimulus this present study would never
have been made. At the same time, attempts to develop
theologies of the various obligations placed on Christians
may fail to indicate the integrated demand the Word of God
places upon his people. We cannot, of course, avoid dealing
with the parts. But we should now and then stand back and
see how the parts fit together. So while this essay shares the
burden of these newer discussions, it seeks to broaden the
horizon to what we might call holistic mission.

Nor must these questions be thought relevant only to
overseas missions. Here in America there is a growing
awareness of the political and social dimensions of our Christian witness. The programs of the Moral Majority and the
writings of Catholic theologian Michael Novack on the one
hand and black and feminist liberation theologies on the
other all testify to the fact that we need to think through our
mission in an entirely new way.

This book attempts to address these questions as a
whole by way of an essay in biblical theology. It seeks to
respond to the fundamental issue: what is the biblical view of
God's mission in the world? It may be that Scripture approached on its own terms, without some preconception
about what "the Church has always believed about evangelism," will clarify the issues. For in Scripture God is obviously interested in the whole person, embedded as he or she
is in the whole of creation and inserted in a particular history. Interestingly enough, while all parties to this discussion acknowledge scriptural authority, few have taken the
time to pursue a thoroughly biblical study of mission.

The Method of Biblical Theology

Since the beginning of this century, a movement of biblical
scholarship has developed under the name "biblical theology." Taking its impetus from the work of Karl Barth (1886-
1968), this movement has found its most important expression in the monumental ten-volume *Theological Dictionary
of the New Testament*, edited by G. Kittel and G. Friedrich.
(The German edition began in 1932, and the English transla-

tion first appeared in 1964.) This approach to theology seeks to study biblical themes in their historical and cultural context as they develop in Scripture. Rather than approaching theology in terms of categories of systematic thought, biblical theology identifies various leitmotivs as they develop in the course of God's dealing with his people. Such an approach is particularly significant for a study of mission because biblical theology deals primarily with God's self-revelation in the course of history and in terms of particularly cultural realities, and encompasses the whole of the biblical record.

Christians who revere the Bible are not always careful about the way they use this record. A "theology of . . . something" becomes very often biblical passages that deal with that issue, or merely "Christian ideas about . . ." A biblical theological approach avoids that error by centering on God's own concern in mission and seeks to see mission as a reflection of his own character and an extension of his creative work. We will seek to use this method in order to come to a fresh reading of Scripture on the subject of mission. For all parties would agree that either the impetus and reality of mission arises from the fabric of Scripture or we are not interested in it.

We need to make two qualifications on the use of this method. First: proponents of biblical theology in recent years have begun to emphasize the great diversity that exists in Scripture, seeking various stands of theological thought—that sometimes oppose one another—in the various books and sections. The reminder of the great diversity of historical and even cultural situations in which the Scriptures were written is a healthy corrective to seeing the Bible as a monolithic unity. The Bible is a genuinely historical and human document that reflects real-life situations. At the same time, it will be an assumption of this essay that there is an overriding unity to Scripture that relates to God's redemptive purposes with his people. Interestingly, many making use of biblical theological methods have held out for a religious unity to the Bible—i.e., a unity of the faith and confession of

Israel or the Church that binds Scripture together (see e.g., Eichrodt).[9] Since the idea of inspiration has been given up by many scholars, they have sought a new unifying factor in the faith of God's people. But this seems to turn matters on their head. How can we speak of a common core of religious experience unless we have first assumed the consistent presence and action of God as the object of this faith? Indeed we believe there is a religious unity to Scripture, but this is because there is first of all a theological unity: God is actively working out his redemptive purposes, and the Bible is the unique and authoritative account of this project. It is this theological unity that the doctrine of inspiration assumes and expresses, and whatever its other virtues no suitable substitute has yet appeared in the biblical theology movement. This weakness is sufficient cause for the supposed crisis of biblical theology spoken of a few years ago (see B. S. Childs).[10]

Secondly: we will follow in general the canonical rather than the historical order of material, thus leaving to one side the question of what critical reconstruction lies behind the present accounts. Thus we will begin with creation, recognizing that it was probably the Exodus experience and the promise to the patriarchs that lies at the beginning of Israel's consciousness; in the New Testament we begin with Christ, even though we know that Paul's letters chronologically came first and that even the synoptic Gospels reflect in some way the experience of the early Church. Even among critical scholars there is an increasing appreciation for the theological significance of the canon as it stands. B. S. Childs comments: "It is only in the final form of the biblical text in which the normative history has reached an end that the full effect of this revelatory history can be perceived."[11] For in the very process of forming the canon, God directed the shape and communication of his redemptive purposes.

This overriding unity of Scripture is best brought out by a careful use of typology wherein correspondences are sought between various events of Scripture. A type is "a biblical event, person or institution which serves as an example or pattern for other events, persons or institutions."[12] In our study we will be alert to correspondences which Scripture highlights and which can help us develop a full-orbed understanding of mission. Because of the consistency of God's purposes, events that find their meaning in God's program can themselves prefigure the future. Not only should verses and passages not be taken out of context, but events and promises as well need to be placed in their larger historical contexts.

Significance of Mission for Theology

Emil Brunner has written that the Church exists by mission as fire exists by burning. Another way of saying this is to point out that theology consists primarily of reflection on mission. This is true on the most basic level: the most highly developed theological statements, those of the Apostle Paul, were forged in the context of the first expansion of the Church.

But this relationship relates also to the nature of theology itself. Mission is not merely an application of theology—something we teach our students after they have learned their theology (though such a Greek separation of theory from praxis has certainly had its influence on our seminaries). But mission lies at the core of theology—within the character and action of God himself. There is an impulse to give and share that springs from the very nature of God and that therefore characterizes all his works. So all that theologians call fundamental theology is mission theology.

But we may go further. Mission is vital to theology because it is the point where faith and strategy come together, where our faith becomes directed toward the world in a specific way. Such a unity follows from the scriptural view of truth which is something to be done and not only believed, and of understanding which follows rather than precedes obedience. In the Bible, knowing God is not a mystical insight but a concrete response to his call. To know

God is to do his will. So we not only can say that good theology will lead to mission, but in biblical mission we are doing theology.

For these reasons, it is not hard to see why questions relating to missions have come to a new prominence recently. Mission leader Emilio Castro in fact has said: "We have seen the end of one missionary era; we are beginning a new one in which the idea of world mission will be fundamental."[13] We can hope that such a consciousness will suggest to churches that they evaluate all their programs missiologically; that they will see their gifts and calling, diverse as they must be in today's complex world, in terms of their primary call to witness in word and deed to the new creation Christ has inaugurated. Surely in the midst of a vigorous and multifaceted witness we can expect an invigorated theology.

Primary Metaphor: Dramatic Action of the Kingdom of God
An image that presents itself as capable of capturing this dynamic aspect of God's action in history is that of dramatic movement. Now very often our thinking about missions is hindered not so much by *what* we think as by the *way* we think. We approach mission either as a body of theory or as a practical strategy, but seldom have notable success in bringing the two together. So on the one hand we are left wondering how we are to put our ideas about mission into practice. Or on the other hand, after snappy short courses on mission or evangelistic methods we are left with a vague and uneasy feeling that we lack biblical warrant for the way we do things. It might be that approaching missions in terms of dramatic movement might help to overcome some of these difficulties.

In the first place drama has the advantage of combining act, speech and setting into one meaningful whole. In a play there is no question about how the acts and dialogue relate to each other, because the unity of the dramatic movement brings them together in an obvious way. A great play makes both movement and speech seem inevitable because all the parts call for each other; the parts lean against each other and throw light on their interlocking meanings. In the same way the setting and props have a part to play—except in some modern plays where the setting almost disappears, but this very lack is part of what the playwright is trying to communicate. In a similar way, in Scripture the acts and speech of God, those of his people and the created context are gathered together and combined into a single whole. Creation itself takes on a role as setting and prop in the drama, and not merely the background for some shadow play.

Dramatic action, incidentally, is far better suited to the emphasis Hebrew thinking places on narrative acts rather than on psychological or theological commentary. Characters—including God himself—are portrayed rather than described, and it is just this quality that is the stuff of great drama. Indeed, Erich Auerbach has shown what an impact the Christian story has had on the development of the dramatic quality of Western literature.[14] And J. R. R. Tolkien has argued: "The gospel contains a fairy story . . . which embraces all the essence of fairy stories. . . . The art of it has the supremely convincing tone of Primary Art, that is of creation. Because this story is supreme, and it is true. Art has been verified. . . . Legend and history have met and fused."[15]

Even more importantly, dramatic movement underlines the fact that we who call on God's name have become actors on the stage and not merely spectators in the galleries. While it is true that some people go through life in a television stupor under the illusion that they are spectators rather than actors in life, in point of fact every one has a part to play—even if some tragically will not realize this until they stand before God to give account of themselves. When playing a role, actors are impelled to say their lines and play their part; the dramatic action forces it upon them. And when the time comes and they stand in their place, they have the feeling that the whole world depends on what they will say. Indeed, the world of the play does "hang" on every word and each action.

Finally: we must not forget that our metaphor allows us to believe that God himself is the chief actor in the drama. We meet with him who calls the world into existence and calls out a people with whom to share his purposes. But this initiative will always be taken in terms of promises and demands that encompass the actors and the setting. As chief actor and playwright, he has conceived a drama that brings all the parts into a meaningful unity. But though he takes the initiative, his actions call for a response. In fact, though one never doubts his Lordship, one often has the feeling that the outcome depends entirely on his people. It is this characteristic that gives scriptural drama its sense of reality. The loving Lordship of God is always exercised in a context that allows for, indeed insists on, the free and fully human response of his people. How this can be we may often wonder, but that it is so we cannot bring ourselves to doubt.

The Unity of the Kingdom of God: The Shape of Mission
Theologically the name of this drama—extending from creation to consummation—is the kingdom of God. We will reflect on the multiplex character of this kingdom and the various aspects it assumes in the history of God's dealings with creation. But as a preliminary definition let us think of the kingdom as God's dynamic rule leading to the salvation of his people and the restoration of the created order. The implications of this category for mission are obvious. For it reminds us that God's· ultimate purpose involves a project combining God, his people and the created order in a single reality in which his glory will be fully and completely manifest.

This unified conception is important because theologians are sometimes better at dividing things up than they are in putting the pieces together afterward. Of course, categories and analysis are important ways of encouraging precision in our thinking. But we need to remember that distinctions, say between the creation and evangelistic mandates or between belief as trust and belief as assent, only describe different dimensions of a specific reality. And when we consider the total program of God, it is the interrelationship that we will want to understand. We must remember at the beginning that God has one purpose in mind: to glorify himself. And though there are many facets, there is only one history of any significance, only one program that God will use to achieve his purpose. As Jose Míguez-Bonino points out:

> God builds his Kingdom from and within human history in its entirety; his action is a constant call and challenge to man. Man's response is realized in the concrete arena of history with its economic, political, ideological options. Faith is not a different history but a dynamic, a motivation, and, in its eschatological horizon, a transforming invitation.[16]

The drama then to which we turn is the story of this kingdom. It is a drama of five acts: creation, exodus, exile, Christ and consummation. These great events, which G. K. Chesterton has called God's gestures in history, comprehend the whole of creation and history. They compose the stage on which we now walk and the final context in which we say our part.

Act One

Creation

When you start writing a story, do you always know what the
end will be?

Yes. I think the end is implicit in the beginning. It must be.
If that isn't there in the beginning, you don't know what
you're working toward. You should have a sense of a story's
shape and form and its destination, all of which is like a
flower inside a seed.

Eudora Welty

Chapter One

Creation of the World

The God who is holy and exalted comes to us and becomes known to us in his creative work. We know him only in these terms, and we serve him only in this context. While God is our final environment, we can only know him in the spatial and temporal forms of his creation. So to understand our role as people called by God, we look first at the creation and see what limits and potential he places there for our service.

Stories and legends of creation exist in many cultures of the world. The most famous are those of the ancient Near East. The great Babylonian *Epic of Creation* begins:

> When the heaven (-gods) above were as yet uncreated,
> The earth (-gods) below not yet brought into being,
> Alone there existed primordial Apsu who engendered them,
> Only Mummu, and Tiamat who brought all of them forth. (1.1)

Then begins the great drama and struggle that resulted in the creation of the Babylonian world. In the midst of all such stories, the biblical account is unique for its simplicity and sobriety. Only the Hebrews remember the past with such clarity and authority. In this first expression of God's dynamic rule there is no struggle with lesser gods, only the simple expression of authority and an emerging order that progressively sets the stage on which the human family will take its place.

God Creates the World

Turning to the first chapter of the Bible we find in verse 1 a summary of all that will be further explained in chapter 1: "In the beginning God created the heavens and the earth." Verse 2 sets the Spirit and darkness over against each other. Rather than echoing some primeval battle with the gods, as some believe, this probably reflects God's normal method of working—from formless to formed. If there is any suspense in the chapter, however, it lies between verses 2 and 3.

There is darkness and the void. There is God. We all know the primitive fear of darkness and the chaos it seems to speak of. The Bible, in fact, later makes use of this apocalyptic theme of the struggle with the powers of chaos and associates it with creation: "Thou dost rule the raging of the sea; . . . the heavens are thine, the earth also is thine; the world and all that is in it, thou hast founded them," says the Psalmist (Ps. 89:9, 11). This creative power is echoed in the Song of Miriam in Exodus 15 and the Song of Deborah in Judges 5, indicating that it is God's creative power that overcomes Israel's enemies and establishes her in the Promised Land. The darkness and earthquake at the crucifixion and the imagery of Revelation reiterate that God's mighty power alone can conquer the forces arrayed against the realization of his kingdom, and that the forces of nature themselves become God's instruments in the struggle for righteousness.

But all of this lies in the future; here all threat of alien forces flies before God's word. "God holds creation," says Gerhard von Rad, "above the abyss of chaos by his word."[1] Verse 3 sets all fears at rest with the refrain, "And God said . . ." This phrase—repeated ten times in Genesis 1— underlines the fact that God's word is the primary means of creation. Indeed, Herman Gunkel points out that "Speech is really the chief medium through which God influences the action in Genesis."[2] Creation then results from the personal communication of God, and in a sense is itself the word of God. That this is more than a metaphor becomes clear in John 1, where John harks back to the Genesis account and speaks of the Word of God as existing in the beginning and constituting the means by which all things exist. And as that Word became flesh in Jesus (John 1:14), so in the beginning the word stands behind the forms of creation and becomes incarnate in that order, an order which provides the meaning that, despite our best scientific efforts, always eludes our perfect human understanding.

The six days of creation are clearly poetic expressions of a real division of ages, and reflect the gradual unfolding of the created order. As man and woman will later be enlisted in the program of creation, so here the processes of life are pressed into service: "Let the earth bring forth . . . Let the waters bring forth." The order reflects the general order envisioned by science, and work begun on the first three days is carried on in days four, five and six. The account recognizes real divisions of time and order within the plant and animal worlds. Each element is given its meaningful place in the order of the whole. Note that God not only expresses his Lordship by the act of creating ("and God said . . . and it was so"), but also by assigning to each element its place and proper designation ("God called the dry land Earth . . . God saw that it was good"). Here is the explicit claim to God's ownership of creation that will be assumed throughout Scripture and that becomes important in any consideration of the stewardship role of man and woman (see Lev. 25:23 and Ps. 24:1).

Creation expresses the fully personal will of God. Notice that this is quite the reverse of the primitive tendency to personify nature, to see in its powers and depths alien forces which must be appeased. The truth is not the personification of nature, but a person creating a world suitable to his personal ends. In fact, many commentators point out how the account goes out of the way to stress that just those heavenly powers often deified or ascribed godlike powers—

sun, moon and stars in verses 14, 15 or the sea monster in
verse 21—are shown to exist at the command of God and
under his Lordship. The creation is demythologized!

God Sees the World

1. *Its goodness*. The world is now given independent existence over against God; though it exists at his will and expresses his purposes, it is not God. Still God sees it—six
times this refrain is repeated ("And God saw . . ."—vv. 4,
10, 12, 18, 21 and 25)—and declares simply: "It is good."
Now this clearly includes the element of God's enjoyment of
creation. The Hebrew "good" has a much broader meaning
than merely ethical and extends to the aesthetic.[3] Surely it
echoes the joy that Scripture elsewhere says accompanied
God's creative work:

> . . . when the morning stars sang together, and all the sons
> of God shouted for joy? (Job 38:7)

But as Claus Westermann points out, goodness includes
more than its objective qualities; it relates to the system of
relationships into which it has been introduced. Creation is
"good or suited to the purpose for which it is being prepared."[4] Now, of course, the final goal of creation lies in the
future; but this end is anticipated in the original character of
things—there is something of realized eschatology here!

In one sense, God's pronouncement has the character
of a promise or, better, a guarantee. This now becomes a
given of creation. The fall, as we will see, introduces the
tragic dimension of disorder and rebellion; but there is no
hint in Scripture that creation's essential goodness is lost
(see Psalm 19:1ff.).

Each creature is assigned its place and reflects the
meaning of the whole. But note that in fulfilling its role in
this order—in simply being itself—it praises God:

> Praise him, sun and moon,
> praise him, all you shining stars!

Praise him, you highest heavens,
  and you waters above the heavens!
Let them praise the name of the Lord!
  For he commanded and they were created. (Ps. 148:3-5)

Once more the theme of the intrinsic joy and delight of creation is sounded: "Praise is joy in a to-God-directed existence, and this joy in existence belongs to creation as a whole."[5]

All of this has great importance for the mission of God's people. For the point of creation's goodness is that God has determined that his glory will be revealed in and through the created order. Its material and organic character not only is no barrier to this glory, but it is hereby pronounced a suitable—even necessary—vehicle thereto. It is hard to escape the feeling that this goodness is of such a foundational character that all the good things that God wills to accomplish in his further purposes must depend on this and grow out of it, even if the new creation will provide a new dimension and the consummation a sublime showcase for this goodness.

2. *Its blessing*. A further element is now added to this goodness when God three times pronounces a special blessing on creation (see 1:22; 1:28; and 2:3).

And God blessed them, saying, "Be fruitful and multiply. . . ." (1:22)

The basic meaning of this blessing to the animals is "the power to be fertile."[6] *Blessing* throughout Genesis is the conferring of beneficial power that produces fertility in men and in livestock and lands.[7] This power will become a very special component of the human ability to grow and subdue the earth, for creation now has been given its unique dynamic: the power of growth and reproduction. This power is operative especially in Genesis 4:17-22 and in chapters 5 and 10, which, we will note, stand in the closest connection to the first three chapters of Genesis. From the beginning the power of growth, which will be used in human projects designed to defy God, and which we think of as natural, even slightly unclean, is pronounced a special blessing. Man and woman are made to share this blessing, which will become foundational for all higher blessings (as that in Genesis 12:3). The third blessing, pronounced in 2:3, speaks of a wholly new relation between God and creation and deserves a separate treatment.

God Rests

The third blessing is tied to the seventh day—the day of completion, in which God rests from his work. The seventh day, we read, is hallowed "because on it God rested from all his work which he had done in creation" (2:3). God has finished his work and declared "it is very good" (1:31). We have reached what Walter Kaiser[8] calls one of the three markers that divide God's creative work. The first declares creation is finished; the second announces the entrance of the new creation, as Christ cries from the cross, "It is finished" (John 19:30); the third proclaims the consummation of the new heaven and new earth, "It is done!" (Rev. 21:6). In each case a significant point has been reached in God's relation with creation, something has been done that cannot now be undone. So God rests.

What sort of rest does God enjoy? It is certainly not a rest of exhaustion, but one of completion, of fulfillment of his purposes; not one of weakness but of power and determination. Moreover, the Scriptures tell us it is God's will that creation itself will share rest. The weekly sabbath which is to be a time of rest and rejoicing becomes for God's people a partial realization of this rest (Ex. 20:8-11); it is associated with the happiness of harvest in the feast of weeks (Deut. 16:9ff.), and with the seventh year of liberation and release of debts (Lev. 25:1-8). But all these pictures, though real blessings in themselves, point to a higher rest which God intends his people to enjoy:

There remains a sabbath rest for the people of God; for

whoever enters God's rest also ceases from his labors as God
did from his. (Heb. 4:9, 10)

Much has to transpire before we see the shape of this rest in
any detail, but we can say here that this rest already exists in
God's relation to the world. Peace already exists because it
reflects his character, because it exists in him, and because
in his freedom he has fulfilled his creative purpose. Though
creation has yet to enter fully into this rest, it is already
there and nothing creation does can disturb that reality.

But God's rest is not a rest of turning away from creation, as though it is of no further concern of his. It is rather a
turning toward creation, for his work always remains open to
him. In a sense, God's rest is a rest of waiting: he waits for
the response of the creature. Remember, God's blessing has
put a power of growth into the order of things. Creation is
not created to stand still, but to develop and grow. In fact,
one could almost say that though creation is good, part of its
goodness lies in what it can become, in the process that God
has initiated. Now something may *happen* in this world; it is
not only sound and fury signifying nothing. Time, which is
created with the world, is not something to flee, but to fill
up. It is itself a potential vehicle of God's presence and
goodness.

Meanwhile, God waits. If creation's glory lies in the
meaning God has implanted in it, the highest end it can
reach is when creation itself perceives that the word that lies
at the basis of everything (Job 28:23 and Psalm 104:9) is
really a call coming to it from God himself. In Proverbs this
order, called wisdom, takes voice and calls:

> Happy is the man who listens to me,
> watching daily at my gates,
> waiting beside my doors.
> For he who finds me finds life. . . .
> All who hate me love death. (8:34-36)

Here already is the echo of the God-man who calls: "Come

to me, all who labor and are heavy laden, and I will give you rest" (Matt. 11:28). To understand how creation may learn to answer this call we must turn to the creation of man and woman.

But before we leave this, we may point out the essential dramatic quality of the situation that lies before us. God waits for a response from his creation. Will there be an answer? What will it be? Already we feel the great question that continues to address people of all ages who live, often unwittingly, in the presence of the waiting God. We feel the intrinsic excitement that accompanies the work of pressing home the claims of God upon a weary and jaded generation.

Implications for Mission

When we speak of beginning, we inevitably deal with creation in its entirety. And when we speak of coming into being, we cannot avoid the question of the meaning of the whole. It is our misfortune to struggle with the pieces; God insists on dealing with the total creation. For the world has been created as an interrelated whole, at every point of which God is immediately concerned. We cannot focus on the importance of any single part without implying the whole, for "just because it belongs to its kind, each individual is directed to the ordered whole, God's creation."[9]

The relation of God to the world is not the relation of a cause to its effect. This is the terrible misstep the pre-Socratics first took and which continues to dog our thinking. The relation is rather one of a personal Creator to his creation. Belief in creation in a biblical sense impels us to recognize that the relation between God and the world is a fully personal one. The Psalmist, after recounting the connection between God and his creatures in a way that seems pantheistic to us ("Thou dost cause the grass to grow") concludes: "May the glory of the Lord endure for ever, may the Lord rejoice in his works" (Ps. 104:31). We speak of personal evangelism, but let us not forget the *personal* interest the Creator takes in all his creatures ("Are not two sparrows sold for a penny? And not one of them will fall to the ground without your Father's will," Matt. 10:29). For as we shall see, there is a clear relationship hinted at in Scripture between human deliverance and the liberation of the creature (Rom. 8:19-21).

This means that this structured order, this multifaceted work of God will always be the basic setting for our mission. As creation was the first expression of God's Lordship, so it will one day in its restored form be the perfect expression of his glory. Meanwhile, the heavens continue to "tell the glory of God" (Ps. 19:1). When Christ tells his disciples to go "into all the world," it is this created order into which he sends us; when he announces, "the meek shall inherit the earth" (Matt. 5:5 and Ps. 37:11), it is this same creation that is offered. It is hard to see how any conception of mission that underestimates this context can be fully biblical. But to understand more clearly this claim we must turn to the creation of man and woman and their fall.

Chapter Two

The Creation of Man and Woman

Introduction

The Genesis account of creation reaches its climax with the account of human creation in 1:26-31. In man and woman and in their life before their Creator, God's highest purposes are both realized and reflected. The most striking thing about the account is the deliberation on the part of God before creation. Whereas previously the text simply states, "God said . . . and it was so," here God says, "let us make man in our image. . . ." Many theologians have insisted we have here clear evidence of God's triune nature. While such an explicit claim may not be warranted, there is at least an echo of the diversity within the Godhead. As Barth noted, "We have to do with a concert of mind and act and action in the divine being itself . . . (with) the one and only God, yet who is not for that reason solitary, but includes in himself the differentiation and relationship of I and Thou."[1]

Such reflection must certainly include the final goal that God envisions in creation. The work of God is oriented toward an end, and this deliberate decision means that the end is now in view: his creature may now become his people. As Paul would later express this goal: God the Father "chose us in (Christ) before the foundation of the world, that we should be holy and blameless before him" (Eph. 1:4). How this high goal is implied in the creation of our first parents it is our job to discover.

Made of Dust

While human creation is preceded by a special deliberation on God's part, it still belongs essentially to the material creation. This is particularly stressed in 2:7 where God forms—the Hebrew word is used of a potter shaping a vessel—man out of the dust from the ground. Though man and woman are blessed with the power of fertility (1:28), even this power is shared with the animals (1:22). Humble beginnings for such a noble creation! Or is this simply our bias against our material context? For there is no hint that such a dimension constitutes a liability for the man and the woman; it has nothing (yet) to do with the fall. To the contrary, in the biblical account this earthly part is considered the natural means by which we are to express our personal life. In fact, it appears that bodily life is uniquely capable of expressing spiritual values, to the extent of voicing God's own glory. The New Testament (referred to as NT from here on) goes so far as to call the body, potentially at least, the temple of the Holy Spirit (1 Cor. 6:19). For a Jew who revered the Temple as the place where God's name dwelt and his glory was visible, this was an amazing claim. Animal impulse and appetite then, which we tend to belittle, are not in themselves a handicap. For this vitality in the Old Testament (hereafter OT) is clearly one of the basic characteristics of the human person, "the individual living being who has neither acquired nor can preserve life by himself, but who is eager for life, (is) spurred on by vital desire."[2]

This interdependence with creation has another component which we must note carefully. It is not possible for this solidarity to be broken. However much they may pride themselves on their independence, people are never "on their own" with respect to their physical environment. We are always dependent on the created order and on others around us. We are utterly dependent on the air we breathe, the water we drink and the food we eat. Nor does it ordinarily occur to us that this is a burden; rather, these elements constitute a part of the delight of being alive. Indeed, this situation should teach us gratitude toward all that we owe to those processes around us which support our life. In the biblical account all this takes on higher meaning when we learn that this dependence expresses and enacts the greater dependence we ought to feel upon God, who lovingly upholds this order with his hand. This reaches the point where the lowliest of elements—the bread and wine—become a symbol of our very communion with God.

So our material and physical life from the beginning form a necessary attendant to all human striving and even our service to God. As W. Eichrodt points out, "Where the unconditional demand of the Creator's will is laid upon the existence of an actual people in its concrete reality, it is not possible for that will to be indifferent to the natural foundations of life."[3] While on the one hand God invites us to share as he rejoices in his works (Ps. 104:31), still he does not forget that we are dust (Ps. 103:14). This is why, as we soon see, in rebelling against the order of things (forgetting we are dust) we not only ruin our lives, but in a sense destroy the earth as well. This is why too the Bible often praises God for his creation and his restoration in the same breath (Ps. 24; 135:6; 147; 148).

Made to Reflect God
It would be a high enough privilege for man and woman to share in God's good purposes for creation. But the accounts make a more far-reaching claim: man and woman are made to reflect God. Formerly the emphasis of theologians has been on human rational and spiritual capacity as the meaning of the "image of God," and surely these are special marks of human life. But in recent years the stress has come to rest on the importance of relationship in the Genesis account. A close look at the record shows this to be an accurate reading. Most important for the human family is its placement in a system of relationships (with each other and with the rest of creation) that in some mysterious way reflects God's own relation to creation.

For on the one hand, though dependent on creation (in this of course we are quite unlike God) we are able to transcend it—"and let them *have dominion*" (1:26). Genesis 2:7 notes God breathed into man the breath of life, clearly involving some special endowment. How may we understand this unique position? By the use of symbols and imagination we are able to anticipate the future, recall the past and transport ourselves into distant times and places. We are able to master our environment by our tools and implements; we are able to shape our communal life by our promises and our institutions. But this very ability to free ourselves from the immediacy of sensation and appetite gives rise to aspirations that the world cannot satisfy. All created things have their place but also, from the human point of view, their limits. In the classic words of Augustine:

> They rise, and set; and by rising, they begin as it were to be; they grow, that they may be perfect; and perfected, they wax old and wither; and all grow not old, but all wither. . . . Thus much hast Thou allotted them, because they are portions of things, which exist not all at once, but by passing away and succeeding, they together complete that universe, whereof they are portions. . . . They rend (the soul) with pestilent longings, because she longs to be, yet loves to repose, in what she loves. But in these things is no place of repose; they abide not, they flee; and who can follow them with senses of the flesh?[4]

Still there is no hint yet of such futility in Genesis 1 and 2, for the man and woman must have known the perfection of God as intimately as they knew the limitation of their environment. Indeed, the latter was for them the condition of the former. In an observation pregnant with implications for our holistic mission, C. N. Krause notes: "Man's capacity for spiritual transcendence is an inclusive cumulative capacity . . . our spiritual personhood is constituted in and through our creaturely existence."[5]

Made to Reflect God by Responding to Him in the Context of Creation

In the account before us it is clear then that the man and

woman reflect God by responding to him. But they do not respond in a vacuum, in some specified religious way, but in the natural context of their created environment. Exactly what the image of God consists in we may leave aside for the moment; what is important for us is that Adam and Eve are called at once to be responsible to God. Professor Eichrodt goes so far as to insist: "The basic phenomenon peculiar to man is consciousness of responsibility."[6] The man and woman are called to do something on behalf of God: to rule and have dominion. This has led Claus Westermann to define the image as relating to the whole of mankind in the whole of his existence. He is created with a purpose: "that something may happen between him and God and that thereby his life may receive a meaning."[7] When this exchange began to take place, then we would be able to see how man and woman reflected God. But what was to happen? Creation was pronounced good; it had already realized what God had in view. But in another sense there remained a higher purpose that God envisioned. In this sense the good of creation was only a potential good. Its real glory would not be seen until someone brought out all that lay buried in its depths—someone had to till and keep it, someone had to tame its abundance. This was to be the fundamental mission of man. Harry Kuitert has captured this responsible dimension of human life well:

> We cannot see God in man while man stands still. To look like God has to do with the purpose God has for man. The question, then, is what is man for, what is his calling? What is he here for? He is here to reflect God, to reflect God the covenant partner. To be God's image means simply that we as men are to live as covenant partners with God and with our fellows on earth.[8]

So the primary import of the image lies in what man and woman are created to do. This mission, as we will see presently, is fundamentally directed toward creation: be fruitful and multiply, have dominion, name. But is not the person created to know God? Where does that come in? The answer is that the first chapters of Genesis are permeated with intimate relationship between the Creator and our first parents. But there is no separate area where this knowledge comes to expression, no special area in which God was known. For from the beginning of Scripture it is clear that it is in our common task as covenant partners with God that we know him. The coming of Christ and the pouring out of the Holy Spirit will add a new and more intimate dimension of this knowledge—an intimacy of course that is not entirely unknown in the OT. But it will remain true that we know God basically in doing his will. We will notice further on how recent scholarship on the knowledge of God in the OT has made it clear that "to know" God means to acknowledge one's loyalty to the covenant relationship and its accompanying demands.[9] So if Adam and Eve are to know God, it will be in an active involvement in God's purposes for creation.

Made to Work on a Common Task
The basic commission given to man and woman—what they are created to do—is given in Genesis 1:28: Be fruitful and multiply, fill the earth, subdue it, and have dominion. To this a further responsibility is added in 2:19, 20: man is to name the animals. Notice that these instructions in 1:28 are premised with a special blessing, a blessing which people share with the animals (cf. 1:22). This basic strength and productivity is now placed in the service of a higher calling. To this blessing is added a special responsibility: they are to rule over creation. They will reflect God's own rule over creation by standing over the order and in their own creaturely way directing its processes. Like God, they are not to be at the mercy of creation, but to share in his own direction of creation toward its goal. This must certainly reflect their creation in God's likeness, for here is "a participation of man in the being and life of God, a willing of what he wills and a doing of what he does."[10]

So the fundamental mission given to man and woman is directed toward creation. As Westermann observes, "Man is created not to minister to the gods, but to civilize the earth."[11] But it is in this fundamental responsibility that the person achieves his or her particular glory. As the Psalmist sings:

> Thou dost crown him with glory and honor.
> Thou has given him dominion over the
>   works of thy hands; thou hast
>   put all things under his feet. (Ps. 8:5, 6)

It is important that we realize that this basic lordship of man and woman is a fundamental responsibility. This clear reflection of God's rule is imaged in the kings of Israel who subdued all her enemies (see 1 Kings 5:4 and Psalm 110:2), and it is applied to the rule of Christ who exercised a greater dominion than that lost in the fall (Matt. 28:18). The Epistle to the Hebrews quotes Psalm 8 and applies it to the suffering and death of Jesus by which he "destroy[ed] him who has the power of death, that is, the devil, and delivered all those who through fear of death were subject to lifelong bondage" (Heb. 2:14, 15; cf. vv. 5-9). It is this reestablished dominion we announce in our proclamation of the gospel. This Lordship of Christ may be more than Adam and Eve's, but it is certainly not less.

Man and woman's authority over creation from the beginning was exercised in the context of interdependence with it. From the outset our fortunes are linked with the soil, and, we are beginning to understand, its fortunes are linked with ours. We can bring out its best or its worst. But though man is put in the Garden to till it (2:15), he is promised ample reward. I have given you, God says grandly, every plant that grows for food (1:29, 30; 2:16). Here the biblical theme of the abundance of God's provision is first sounded. The man and woman are placed—to play or dance one feels rather than to work—in the midst of all that is lovely and pleasant (2:8, 9). Creation offered plenty to meet the needs and desires of God's children. There would be no want; it had only to be tended and harvested.

But note that in its very temporality another dimension of human responsibility is apparent. The fruits of creation grow to be enjoyed and shared; they cannot be held and hoarded. They will spoil; later moth and rust will corrupt and thieves will steal. Meanwhile, all is given in trust and people are stewards, not the final owner, destined to give account of how creation's bounty was used in those precious moments before its usefulness was gone. Here a call to decision is built into the created order wherein doing nothing becomes a moral decision. Christ later calls the rich man a fool who presumes on all the produce his barns could hold (Luke 12:20); "but happy is he who is kind to the poor" (Prov. 14:21).

The account in 2:18ff. places the man's call to name creation in the context of his search for someone to share his world. All the animals were brought before him, and whatever he called them that was their name (2:19). Here is a further reflection of God's likeness, for God's prerogative to designate the meaning of aspects of creation (1:14 *et al*) is shared by humanity. Naming, the fundamental activity of all science, expresses the man and woman's personal rule over the created order and orientates them in its diversity. For all the joy of naming and taming the teeming vitality of nature, something was lacking—"there was not found a helper fit for him" (2:20b). Do we hear an echo here of God's own desire for fellowship with his creation?

Made to Work Together

Just as a person cannot reflect God while standing still, so he or she cannot reflect God alone. The active concrete call to involvement in God's purposes is always a social call. The summary in 1:27—"Male and female he created them"—is again filled out with the account in 2:20-25. We are made to live in relationship, and we simply cannot exist as human by ourselves. The "helper" that God provides for man is someone to stand over against him—literally a power equal to him[12]—to complement him and provide for herself and for him the opportunity of mutual fulfillment.

The connotation of "helper" underlines the fact that the basic thrust of social obligation is mutual service. This fundamental calling to ministry is highlighted in the ministry of Christ who gave himself to others (Mark 10:45). Each person is incomplete without the other, and while this certainly does not imply that unmarried people cannot be fulfilled, it does mean that life in its fullness must include heterosexual relations in the broad sense. This sexual duality, in fact, Karl Barth believes to be the basic meaning of the image of God. Certainly he is right when he notes that "in faith and love man responds, (man) corresponds, to what is simply the work of God for him and to Him."[13]

From this basic relation grow all the social groupings which define the nature of humankind. Not only is the family the basic social unit, but all larger communities aspire to reflect the openness and sharing of this relationship. In fact, in the NT God's ideal community, the Church, is often called his family wherein all share jointly a common spiritual affinity and as brothers and sisters together call God Father.

This then is the commission given to man and woman: to serve creation and one another in their daily work, to build a social world centering on the family. All these tasks, however humble, have their intrinsic value. All of this done with integrity glorifies God, or at least God cannot be glorified if all this is left undone. Here are Adam and Eve in God's own garden. This is not yet the promised land, but it is at least a land of great promise.

Chapter Three

The Fall and Expulsion from the Garden

Living under God's Instructions

In chapter 3 of Genesis the man and woman stand open before God and each other amidst the munificence of creation. This is a fully personal context in which nothing is fixed—anything is possible. Since their relationship with God continues to be a completely personal and intimate one, Adam and Eve had to live to God freely and intelligently. The rest of creation perhaps followed by instinct God's will; the man and woman needed more explicit instructions. The idea of "instruction" (which is the English translation of the Hebrew word "*torah*" or law) will become important later in the OT record. But already God provided a reminder for his creation that they must live by his word and enjoy creation on his terms.

His first word is one of permission: "You may freely eat of every tree of the garden" (2:16). This was already implied, as we observed, in 1:29 and 2:9. Interestingly the phrase "pleasant to the sight and good for food" in 2:9 is the same as that in 3:6 describing the tree in the midst of the garden. It was not the forbidden fruit that was a delight to the eye (how many sermons have you heard along this line?), but all the trees. All the trees are lovely and useful, God said, and you may enjoy them all.

But the tree in the midst of the garden they were not to eat or they would surely die (2:17). Why does God make such a restriction? Some have speculated that God is testing Adam and Eve and providing them the opportunity of proving their faithfulness and thus reaching a higher stage in their relationship. However this may be, God is clearly setting a boundary around his fellowship with man and woman. They must know that they were not lords absolutely, but only by his permission, and that he would establish the limits of their commission. But notice that such limits, and laws generally in the OT, are not a barrier to fellowship with God but a definition and protection of that fellowship. For life before God is always a responsible one, demanding a particular behavior that expresses the character of that relationship. Understanding this will make it easier for us to see later that keeping the law was never meant to be a means of establishing a relationship with God; rather it is a way of demonstrating that communion once the way is opened for relationship from God's side. God's instructions here express his mercy. As Westermann observes, "The intention of the command is to connect man with God in his daily life in a special way."[1] Many theologians have called this the covenant of works, and the idea of covenant is certainly implicit in this exchange. But it is well to remember that God has placed man and woman from the beginning in a position of responsibility to him, and this command simply makes that reality explicit. It is the human glory to hear the order in which we are made to live spoken in loving invitation.

Hearing the Tempter's Suggestion

The serpent is introduced in 3:1 simply as: "more subtle than the beasts of the field" (which is probably the best translation of this expression[2]). Beyond this we know nothing of this next member of our dramatis personae, and in all likelihood neither did Adam or Eve. He simply appears to innocently inquire about God's instructions—first by challenging God's promise, then daring to contradict it. In such pastoral simplicity who could have guessed the dreadful issue of such casual questions? Who could possibly have known how creation itself was hanging by a thread and that the offhand remarks of the serpent would begin a skirmish that leads to a mighty crashing battle in the final chapters of Revelation? Yet as Proverbs reminds us, life is very much like this: a casual remark, a misstep begins a way that leads to death.

Who is this creature anyway? The entire Scripture sheds scant light on this figure. We suppose it is Satan disguising himself (Paul hints at this in 2 Corinthians 11:3, 14 and Romans 16:20 and John develops the idea in Revelation 12:9 and 20:2). But here we can only say that the questioning comes from creation itself, from a figure that has set itself against the good purposes of God.

The progressive unfolding of forces that withstand God's kingdom will be an increasingly significant factor in our story of God's mission in the world, and it may not be amiss to make some initial observations. First, it must be recognized that besides the many ministering angels, various gods or spirits with real power are acknowledged to be part of the created order. These forces appear on a continuum from persons who are used by evil forces to stand against God to actual appearances of Satan himself (presumably) in human form. They are usually identified with the gods of the neighboring nations or sometimes with the power of chaos within creation itself. In every case however, they are something over which God is seen to triumph by his mighty power. The contest between these forces and God comes to clear expression in Elijah's encounter on Mount Carmel, but is implied in the struggles of Exodus 15 and Psalm 89. By the time of the prophets the pagan gods are accounted as nothing (Isa. 44:9ff.), which surely means that they offer no threat to God's purposes rather than that they have no reality.

The impression is even given that whatever spirits exist are so completely under God's authority that they can be sent to accomplish his purposes, as in the case of the spirits sent to torment Saul. This, of course, is even clearer in the ministry of Christ where the spirits acknowledge his divine Lordship by appealing to him to direct them in specific ways (Luke 8:31).

One should not conclude, however, that the forces opposing God may simply be ignored. Indeed, there is a growing importance given to them in Scripture until we come to the close of Revelation where the struggle of Eden reaches its horrible conclusion in the final battle between the beast and the forces of righteousness (Rev. 19). But even during the ministry of Christ the spirits began to array themselves against God's kingdom and were acknowledged as belonging to the prince of this world (John 12:31); all these, however, were decisively defeated at the cross (Col. 2:15).

But the promise given in Genesis 3:15 proves to be the decisive assurance: though these forces will prove painful, though there will be casualties, they will not prevail. God's power can be challenged; it can never be threatened. In fact, the basic impression one has in reviewing the biblical data is the casual attitude toward all of this. This is all the more surprising since peoples all around Israel (and the New Israel!) lived in constant fear of the powers. The biblical God makes all such fear unnecessary, and it appears that as a result the scriptural record simply does not deign to give the matter any lengthy attention.

But this is not to deny the importance of the drama taking place in the garden. In one sense everything was hanging on the response of Eve, at least as far as she was concerned. Creation must have held its breath. In the words of John Milton:

> Fixed on the fruit she gazed, which to behold
> Might tempt alone; and in her ears the sound
> Yet rung of his persuasive words, impregned
> With reason, to her seeming, and with truth. . . .
> Forth reaching to the fruit, she plucked, she eat.
> Earth felt the wound, and Nature from her seat,
> Sighing through all her works, gave signs of woe
> That all was lost.[3]

The Fall and the Judgment

As the woman is not made to live alone, so she cannot sin alone: "She took of its fruit and ate; and she also gave some to her husband. . . . Then the eyes of both were opened" (3:6, 7). And it did not stop with them, for we are all implicated in their sin. The progress of their sin is made horrifyingly clear in the chapters of Genesis that follow, as the family, society, culture and finally the whole world is infected with their tragic illusions.

The tempter's basic ploy was to induce them to imagine that they could deal with the world on their terms, not, as it is, a being-to-God. "You shall be as gods," could well be the theme of the first eleven chapters of Genesis, as the social shame and religious fear of these chapters works its way into the fabric of civilization.

What will be God's response to this challenge? His first word is a simple question: Where are you?—indicating that easy fellowship with God is now gone, but that the loving God still seeks his people. Then he responds in the form of a promise, or a series of promises, reflecting his judgment upon their sin. As we have seen, God is both a holy and a loving God, so that his judgment always has this dual character of wrath and mercy, of punishment and help. We will see throughout Scripture that his redemptive work now must not only defeat his enemies but also save his creation (and especially those faithful to his word. See Isaiah 10:24-27 and 1:25, 26). This double-sided work is evident already in these verses.

First he promises enmity between the seed of the woman and the seed of the serpent. Notice that "seed" is part of the original blessing of creation, but now it will carry a new and greater potential, that of victory over evil. A struggle is promised, with suffering on both sides, but with a guaranteed victory for the seed of the woman. God's mercy is clear not only in the promise of victory but also in the assurance of enmity; mankind will be unable to make any permanent alliance with evil, even though individual allegiance must be declared for one side or the other.

Secondly the woman is cursed at the fundamental level of family relations and pain in childbirth. Shame already had led to accusations and self-defense (3:10, 12, 13). Now those activities which bring the greatest delight will also reflect the heavy yoke of sin. The fully personal relations within the home, which were meant to reflect God's own intimacy with himself, give way to dominance and subjugation; pain invades the birth-couch.

Finally the earth is cursed "on account of" or "for the sake of" the man. His dominion is not lost, but it will be forever challenged. His rule must be constantly fought for and regained at great cost—sweat, toil, thorns. And the end of it will be death, a final humiliating return to the ground from which he came.

Since the basic sin was a disobedience of God's instructions, a refusal to acknowledge their assigned place in creation, the result was that the proper system of relationships was lost and the balance was upset. Notice that the essential goodness of creation was not lost altogether; it can still be a vehicle of God's glory. But the order was fatally disturbed, and since the whole makes a single interrelated environment, the results had to reach to the meanest creature. Since the structural laws of creation resulted from and reflected God's word (as the NT reminds us, Christ the living word was himself the mediator of creation, Colossians 1:15-19), disobedience can never be a private affair. My disobedience will destroy me, but it will also destroy my family and my community, and ultimately, if God does not intervene, it would destroy the world as well. This is seen today in the widely announced shortages in primary resources. In actuality of course these shortages ordinarily do not reflect a lack of resources but only distorted and greedy patterns of use. But this was already seen in the Old Testament. Sin defiles the land (Deut. 24:4), and disobedience is reflected in the barrenness of the land (Deut. 28), so that the land must vomit out its evil inhabitants (Lev. 18:25, 28). We will notice further on that this defilement comes to clear expression at the death of Christ when darkness covers the land and the earth shakes. For the victory over sin and death, won on the cross and seen in the resurrection, must eventually involve nothing less than the transformation of the created order. For this consummation the creature waits with eager longing (Rom. 8:19-21). Since this is so, salvation can never be a private affair; the world literally hangs on the question of a person's allegiance. And mission must certainly direct itself to this broader dimension.

Man and Woman Are Expelled from the Garden

The curses are climaxed by God putting Adam and Eve out of the garden of Eden. They cannot enjoy the special place which God has made for them without also enjoying his personal presence, for these were made to complement each other. And the way back is barred. Now the hope for mankind is not back to some supposed primitive paradise, but ahead through the further acts of deliverance that God will bring about. But notice that Adam and Eve carry with them the original blessings of creation and its calling; they cannot escape these and remain human. So in 4:1 Eve gives birth and exclaims: "I have gotten a man with the help of the Lord." Perhaps she thought it was the seed that was promised her in 3:15.

But they carried with them also the curse that had been placed upon them. And here the organic connection of these first chapters of Genesis must be noted. Both the blessing and the curses of Genesis 1—3 are extended throughout the earth in Genesis 4—11. All the evil and greatness of fallen humanity, still bearing the image of God, is seen in these accounts. Cain offers his sacrifice to God, but since this is not an expression of genuine worship, he kills his brother when it is refused. The close relation of chapters 3 and 4 is underlined by the question of 4:9—"Where is Abel your brother?" For as Adam and Eve's sin broke the harmony between them and God, so the bond between brother and brother is also torn. Little wonder that later the central commands—love God with your heart, and your neighbor as yourself—are said to hold up the entire law (Matt. 22:40).

Now God's judgment must be felt again. Cain is put out of God's presence and made to wander, even as a mark of protection is put on him (4:15).

But the blessing of creation and the power of growth which expresses that blessing continue to operate. Genesis 4:17-26 shows the work of the growing human family and the beginnings of culture, art and technology. All of this continues to express man's creation in God's image and evidences God's goodness. At the same time, all that is done now bears the mark of human sin. For that sin which was conceived in the heart in chapter 3 bears fruit in society and its structures and institutions in chapter 4. Lamech perverts the role of government by boasting of his rule and his cruel vengeance (4:23, 24); meanwhile Seth is born and "men began to call upon the name of the Lord" (v. 26).

The Human Family Grows and Spreads into All the World
Again the blessing of growth and productivity is expressed in the repeated genealogies of chapter 5, as the descendants of Adam grow and extend their influence. But now a melancholy note intrudes: the refrain "and he died." Now the blessing is borne by one who must die. Similarly a kind of explosion of evil accompanies this growth, which is summarized in chapter 6: "Every imagination of the thoughts of (man's) heart was only evil continually" (6:5). These "heroes," desirous to make a name for themselves, call themselves "sons of god" (perhaps after the Near Eastern fashion),[4] and bring about a great wickedness. But already a helper had been born, a "son" who, it was said, would "bring us relief" (5:29). Here is the first expression of God's deliverance, which characteristically begins with a single individual who "finds favor" in God's sight (6:8). Anticipating too God's later custom of taking the prophets into his confidence before executing judgment, he tells Noah that he will destroy this people. We noticed above how close the language of creation and judgment are in Scripture, and here too the power and terror of great waters spreading over the face of the earth speak of the fact that while God is Creator he can

also be the destroyer of the earth. Evil had reached such proportions that the earth could not simply survive as it was.[5] People will have an end—they will return to dust—and the interlude can only be a period of preservation. So the rainbow is given as a sign of God's promise that he will not destroy every creature as he had done (8:21), a promise that is repeated as a covenant in 9:8ff. But the interim is a continual reminder of his mercy; we can never presume upon it.

What now will the human task be in this interim? The answer is found in 9:1-7, which repeats the commission to Adam and Eve in 1:28ff.: they are to be fruitful, and every living creature is delivered into their hand. Whatever is to happen, the mission of Noah and his descendants is once again tied up with the fortunes of the earth and God's promises to it. Though God makes the covenant with Noah, it is for the sake of the whole earth. Shem is further promised the special presence of God—"let (God) dwell in the tents of Shem," 9:27—which hints of the special blessing that will come to the world through the Semite peoples.

Again like a refrain the blessings of creation are expressed in the genealogies of chapter 10, which this time includes territorial expansion. These verses emphasize the fact that all peoples belong to a single family (11:1), so that, as W. Eichrodt points out, Israel can claim no inherited nobility.[6] However widespread the family of nations, they belong to a common stock and stand on an equal footing before God. But sadly chapter 11 dramatizes how all together they pursue their perverse projects. They pursue the empty promise of the serpent, "you will be as gods," as they seek pitifully to make a name for themselves. So God again comes to judge and scatter them over the face of the earth.

The stage is now set for God's program of restoration. These eleven chapters play a crucial role in the record, for they lay a grand stage for God's work. These chapters paint a broad picture of beginnings and give a multifaceted perspective of the world. They portray a kind of mission in reverse wherein men and women go into all the world in pursuit of the evil projects which fire human imaginations. The sin that entered in chapter 3 has penetrated into every corner of the world and into all human institutions. Since, however, it is still God's creation and continues to share its interrelated character, we will see that God cannot work on a part without taking the whole into account. And it is the whole that concerns God, to the smallest part. For this reason Abram is called out of Ur and sent on a mission.

Chapter Four

The Call of Abraham

Has God Rejected His Creation?

The story we have been following recounts a familiar moral inertia; things often seem to grow worse. Moral failures seem to feed on themselves. Now, however, a note is struck that makes the reader take notice. Things take a wholly different turn. Though the stage has been set, one can almost say the *story* which we intend to follow really begins here. We have seen evil and judgment and the inevitable scattering of peoples (will the stream of refugees ever stop?). Now something happens; a train of events is set in motion that "unexpectedly seizes people out of the history of expulsion and initiates them into a history of anticipation."[1] We have seen destruction; it is said we even get used to it, watching all those violent movies. Now there is hope of a construction, which later will be called "the city . . . whose builder and maker is God" (Heb. 11:10). We have seen aimless wandering; now we are able to imagine a pilgrimage. The narrative of Genesis gathers speed, even as it narrows its focus. A train of events is being set in motion that is now irreversible and that will have universal consequences. All eyes are fixed upon it. These are not stories with a moral, but events with a great moral consequence.[2] Though this initiative is not strictly speaking the beginning of mission, it does inaugurate the redemptive movement of which missions is the final extension. And its character influences the content of our evangel irrevocably.

With the Promise to Abraham God Addresses Himself to the Whole Creation

When we turn to chapter 12 of Genesis we note again that God has to take the initiative and intervene. The narrator is quite laconic about this aspect of the account. The beginning reminds one of the creation account with its simplicity:

> Now the Lord said to Abram, 'Go from your country. . . .'
> (12:1)

> And God said, 'Let there be light.' (1:3)

But the record makes plain that everything depends now on what God will do. From a human point of view there seems no way out. The line of Shem laid out in chapter 11 has led us to someone named Abram, but we learn that "Sarai (his wife) was barren; she had no child" (11:30). The blessing of an heir was conspicuously lacking. So God again speaks, and once again his word becomes the mediator of his presence. Abraham's journey becomes an incarnation of the power of God's word which does not return unto him void.[3]

From a human point of view Abram did not have much to commend him. He belonged to a loose group of nomad clans called "Apiru" (from which comes the name Hebrew) that were making a nuisance of themselves as robbers and brigands in Babylonia in the late third and early second millennium B.C. They were traveling merchants whose name meant "the dusty ones" and was earned from having to walk along the dusty caravan routes behind their donkeys.[4] As God originally made man from the dust, so he will make his special people in a similar way.

Professor Albright believes the reference to Simeon and Levi in Genesis 49:5-7 preserves a very ancient and accurate characterization of these people:

Simeon and Levi are brothers; weapons of violence are their
swords . . . in their anger they slay men, and in their wan-
tonness they hamstring oxen. Cursed be their anger for it is
fierce.

There were extensive caravan routes in this period stretch-
ing between Sudan and Egypt in the south, Asshur and
Cappadocia in the north. Abram can be identified as simply
a "wealthy caravanner and merchant whose relations with
the native princes and communities were fixed by contracts
and treaties (covenants)."[5] So it was in such an inauspicious
setting that God came to Abram and said, "I will make my
covenant between me and you" (17:2).

Interestingly, in chapter 11 when we meet Abram, he
is already in motion, as it happens, toward Canaan. Abram
was already moving, just as everyone else in those early
chapters: plenty of movement, no progress. But now God
gives his journey direction and a goal. Canaan, which Abram
surely had passed through many times, now will be the goal
and not only a stopover. But far more important than the
journey is the promise attending the destination.

This promise now dominates the entire narrative up to
the end of Genesis. In fact David Clines has recently argued
that it gives impetus to the entire Penteteuch,[6] and Gerhard
von Rad places the credo that recounts Abraham's experience in Deuteronomy 26:5 at the center of the first seven
books.[7] The promise, though repeated and elaborated
throughout the patriarchal narratives, contains basically
three elements which we need to discuss: posterity, relation
with God and the land.

1. *Posterity*. God says to Abraham in 12:2, "I will make
of you a great nation," which is elaborated in 15:5 as more
than the stars of the sky (cf. 17:6). Here the fundamental
blessing of creation—seed—is repeated in a new context
that surely harks back to God's promise to the woman in
3:15. But this nation (nations?) will be different; it will be the
means of blessing the whole earth, for it bears a new hope

that promises to set aside the effects of the curse. Reading the various promises to Abram (now called Abraham, "the father of a multitude"), one wonders whether in fact this will really be one nation, or many nations that become one. We will notice often in our study how open to traffic is the boundary between Israel and the nations. One suspects that Israel as a nation was meant in some sense to attract and eventually absorb the other nations.

2. *Relation with God*. The central promise of the patriarchal age is a special relation with God himself: "I will establish my covenant between me and you and your descendants after you . . . to be God to you and to your descendants" (17:7, 8). Again the promise of relationship with God is for the descendants and is surely implied in the blessing that Abraham is to be to all nations (12:3). Here also the election of Israel is not meant to be for Israel only but for all nations. Israel is both a recipient and a mediator of blessing.

3. *The land*. Though mentioned first in 12:2, we place it last as it is in 17:8 for reasons we will discuss shortly. A people cannot live without a land, a special place in which they can express themselves and worship the Lord. Here too the original created purposes for man and woman are recalled wherein they reflect God in their common task in the context of creation. Throughout all ages the land continues to be fundamental to the consciousness of humanity, and if they are to bear God's special blessing it will have to be in some created context.

Now we have formulated the promise in this form because, following Clines, we believe that it expresses what will be the content of the remainder of the first five books. The promise serves as the impetus for the movement of all these books. Genesis is concerned essentially with four figures in succession: Abraham, Isaac, Jacob and Joseph. That is, Genesis 12—50 has primarily to do with the posterity that is promised to Abraham. The next two books, Exodus and Leviticus, have to do with the establishing of the relationship between God and his people, which is expressed both in his delivering and his giving the law. Then Numbers and

Deuteronomy register movement toward the land. Deuteronomy closes with God's people poised ready to possess the land. But as Clines points out,[8] these books give us only a partial fulfillment, and a precarious one at that. For Genesis ends with Joseph being placed in a coffin in Egypt; Leviticus gives us no hint whether these laws will be kept; and Deuteronomy ends with the death and burial of Moses (outside the land). Will God's promises finally prevail? A moment's reflection on the book of Judges and the anointing of Saul only adds to our perplexity. Are these leaders really fulfilling God's program? But these five books also show that despite the failing of God's people, God's promises will not fail. There is actual fulfillment in these books.

This lesson is particularly poignant in Genesis. For just at the aspect of the promise where the narrative focuses—descendants—the challenge is the strongest. Three times women, mothers of the awaited offspring, are put in jeopardy by the hasty lies of a husband (chapters 12, 20, 26). In every case brothers, the hoped for seed, quarrel bitterly and raise the question of Cain: am I my brother's keeper? Then Abraham is asked to sacrifice the son of promise (chap. 22). Finally a famine in the land (the promised land of blessing!) threatens God's people with starvation and sends Jacob's family to Egypt to live on the hospitality of a foreign ruler. In the end the family numbering some seventy persons is left in Egypt, and God's promise has been kept. But for the fullness of this to be seen we must have the events that cement the special relation between God and his people and the land that he has prepared for them.

Before we turn to these themes, however, two questions—important to our reflection on mission—remain to be answered. First, how is it that God can reach the world through one people? Why does he not reveal himself to all? Here we meet God's strange habit of narrowing the focus of his word in order to extend the range of his blessings. As David Clines points out, the universal scope of Genesis 1—11 led to a universal judgment; the narrowing now will lead to blessing for all nations.[9] How can this be? Certainly a part of the answer lies in the organic character of the human race that we have discussed earlier. Lesslie Newbigin in discussing these things points out that in contrast to Christianity, the Hindu view of man believes people exist as isolated spiritual monads. If that were true God would have to reveal himself to each individual for them to find salvation. God's desire, he points out, is not the salvation of persons, but of people, a new humanity. Thus he had to start with one person and one family to be the vehicle of a new collective reality.[10] But the one family could not live except as a servant of others, and Israel had to learn that this was a part of the meaning of the promise. For this to be made clear, however, we have to await the one who came not to be ministered unto but to minister, and who in being lifted up from the earth would draw all men unto him.

But this brings us to our second question: What really was Abraham's part in all this? In one sense, of course, he could do nothing about the promises he was given. His new name must have been an embarrassment to him: father of many nations (Abraham, when will your first nation be born?). And how could he take possession of the land—so carefully ruled and guarded by treaties and alliances? But in another sense everything seemed to hang on his response. He was asked to circumcise his male children, even to be willing to give up his son. All of this gave evidence of his basic confidence in taking God at his word, which was counted to him as righteousness (15:6). His confidence was expressed in his obedience. The substance of the obedience God desired is clarified later in the law, but even at this point we should not underestimate its importance. Throughout Scripture those who would share in God's blessing must "hear" God's promise and keep it. God would keep his promise but his people must keep his word, and the guarantee of that for us rests in the fact that Jesus Christ the covenant-keeper was perfectly obedient to the Father. As for Abraham's children, they could never presume on their physical descent—was his notorious background something to boast of in any case?—for God could raise up children of

Abraham from the stones, as John the Baptist reminded his hearers. But children of Abraham there will be, for the blessing must reach to the ends of the earth.

So though God's concern is with the whole, he begins with one people. "What God did, what he does, and what he will do toward and within his people is always related to the other people, too, even if this relationship is mostly hidden from us."[11] These promises then will echo over vast periods of time and reach to all the nations. They will be as universal as the growth of evil on the earth had been, and their issue will transcend even that bitter reach. On the one hand, they reach back and gather up the creation promises for blessing, for rule and for relationship; on the other hand, they anticipate the great command of Christ that concentrates the reality of his whole life and ministry—to extend his own rule by discipling all the nations of the earth. The historical form that these promises will take becomes clearer as we turn now to the second great act of God's drama: the Exodus.

Act Two

The Exodus

I shall ride the storm
   Tame the waves
Slay the sharks
   I shall drive away the enemy
To save our people.
   I shan't be content with the
Customary fate of women
   To bow their heads as concubines.
—Asian Peasant Woman, 300 A.D.

Chapter Five

The Rescue of God's People

God Hears the Cries of His People

When Joseph died in Egypt, there were not many who
would have put much hope in his family. If they expected
that Joseph was one of the kings who would come out of
Abraham, they were disappointed. But Exodus picks up the
theme of posterity precisely where Genesis leaves off:
though Joseph dies, the family increases until they become
strong and fill the land (Ex. 1:7). But they are still exiles,
foreigners. And they soon become aware of this as a new
ruler arises that "did not know Joseph"—which probably
refers to the native Egyptian rulers freed from the yoke of
the foreign Hyksos rulers who would have been more
favorably disposed to the Hebrews. In three stages the context for God's mighty intervention is laid out.

First God's people become oppressed. The new rulers
dreaded this large unruly mob and set them to work "with
rigor" (1:14). They further made sure they would not increase in number and strength by killing all the male children (no more seed!). We must be careful not to underestimate the importance of this situation of slavery and oppression. For in the first instance the Exodus is clearly a judgment on the wickedness of the Egyptian rulers. We will
discuss this below, but it cannot be denied that God's deliverance of his people is in the first place a social and political upheaval that delivered a helpless slave people from the

hand of oppressive rulers. We see the importance of this in the law, which so often harks back to this fact, and in the refrain of praise for God's righteous deliverance in the worship of Israel. They could sing, "I know that the Lord maintains the cause of the afflicted" (Ps. 140:12) because God had delivered his people from bondage.

But secondly there is a new element added: the cry of the people (2:23). God has now created a people that can appeal to him and cry out in their distress. This cry will be progressively important in the history of God with his people until in the Psalms of lament Israel cries out as a people to God, and Christ on the cross actually takes up this cry (from Ps. 22) and speaks it for and with his people. This all suggests that the relationship that God intends to develop with his people is a fully personal one which therefore allows for human expressions of grief and distress. Indeed Israel would come to know God precisely in this dialogical history of God with his people, through their cries and his answer.[1] This is further explained in Exodus 4:22, 23 when God calls Israel his firstborn for whom he cares as a Father.

But thirdly God hears the cry of his people in remembrance of his promise to the Fathers (2:24; 3:6; 6:8). The impetus for God's actions on behalf of his people continues to be the promise which he made to Abraham. The personal guarantee which God gave with creation, and which has been reiterated to Abraham, now begins to produce its fruit and issue; as God's word it will accomplish that for which it is sent.

God Calls a Man to Announce and Direct His Deliverance

Moses, with his Egyptian name and background,[2] was uniquely prepared by God to deal with the Egyptian rulers. H. H. Rowley has claimed that Moses in a sense was the first missionary in the OT, because God sent him not only to deliver Israel but to lead them to the proper worship of God.[3] Part of his mission, Rowley goes on to note, is expressed in the indignation which he feels against the injustices of his people (Ex. 2:11-13), which, as in the case of

Amos, clearly expressed the indignation of God himself. Whether Moses can properly be called a missionary or not, he certainly begins the office of the prophet who, following an encounter with God (Num. 12:6-8), speaks the word of God to his people, and not only speaks this word but helps to initiate and incarnate the reality of that word in his ministry (see Deut. 18:15-22).

Notice particularly that all God revealed to Moses focused on the establishment of a relationship between God and his people, which now becomes the central theme of the narrative. God reveals to Moses a new understanding of his presence in the formula, "I am who I am" (Ex. 3:14). Although the subject of much discussion, this phrase probably means: "I will be there for you." That is, you can be sure of my presence, which I will demonstrate to you by my actions on your behalf.[4] Then God makes clear to Moses the purpose of his intervention for his people: that they will be able to worship him (3:12; 7:16; 8:1, 20; 9:1; and 10:26). Finally he reveals to him the structure that this relationship is to take in the formal covenant which he makes with them (19:4-6).[5]

Moses then is to be the mediator of God's further elaboration of his promise to Abraham, even as he becomes representative of the kind of person-to-person relationship that God desires for all his people: "With him I speak mouth to mouth, clearly, and not in dark speech; and he beholds the form of the Lord" (Num. 12:8). In the golden calf incident Moses even has to intercede with God to spare the people (Ex. 32:30-35). Here emerges the contour of God's messenger who not only bears but embodies the truth God intends to communicate.

God Acts to Call a People to Himself

After a protracted contest with the magicians of Egypt— "But the magicians of Egypt did the same by their secret arts"—the struggle reaches the point that the magicians could no longer equal the power of God. Interestingly the magicians turn to Pharaoh and confess at that point, "This is the finger of God" (8:19). But Pharaoh continues to harden his heart. And God finally has to send his angel to slay the firstborn son of every family. The judgment of God then reaches to the central promise of seed, and as they had sought to destroy the sons of Israel so they are destroyed. But Israel is saved because the angel of the Lord passes over the houses of Israel with the blood smeared on the doorposts. So at the very center of God's calling out of his people stands the reminder that they cannot know him without the ransom by the payment of a price. This great beginning for Israel (see 12:1ff.) opens with a mighty act of God, but also with a merciful turning away and passing over their sin.

Just as God had shown his superiority over the gods of the nations, and his Lordship over sin, now he triumphs over the forces of chaos, and the pursuing armies of Pharaoh are engulfed. Recalling the waters and floods of creation, the flood and the scattering of Babel, God now delivers his people by his mighty hand. This creationlike event is celebrated in the ancient psalm of Moses in Exodus 15:

> I will sing to the Lord, for he has
>   triumphed gloriously;
> the horse and his rider he has thrown
>   into the sea.
> The Lord is my strength and my song,
> and he has become my salvation;
> this is my God, and I will praise him,
> my father's God, and I will exalt him.
>   (15:1, 2)

And in the still more moving words of Psalm 18:

> In my distress I called upon the Lord;
>   to my God I cried for help.
> From his temple he heard my voice,
>   and my cry to him reached his ears.
> Then the earth reeled and rocked;
>   the foundations also of the mountains
>   trembled

And quaked because he was angry.
  Smoke went up from his nostrils,
and devouring fire from his mouth;
  glowing coals flamed forth from him. . . .
He rode on a cherub, and flew;
  he came swiftly upon the wings of
    the wind. . . .
He brought me forth into a broad place;
  he delivered me, because he delighted
    in me. (Ps. 18:6-8, 10, 19)

Here reference to Exodus is linked in its images to both the beginning and end of creation, so decisive was God's intervention on behalf of his people. Here is a decisive victory of God over all the false gods and the forces threatening the created structure. Surely now Israel will acknowledge forever their gratitude to God. But the narrator wishes to remind us of the reality of their unbelief, when, immediately following this great hymn, they begin to complain. They have no water; they do not have enough to eat; they prefer meat instead of manna. In each case God answers their cry and gives them what they desire, though they suffered for their lack of faith. As the Psalmist recounts: "But they soon forgot his works; they did not wait for his counsel. But they had a wanton craving in the wilderness, and put God to the test in the desert; he gave them what they asked, but sent a wasting disease among them" (106:13-15). As they followed the ancient caravan routes to Kadesh-Barnea, they were bearers of a new treasure, the recipients of God's saving activities. But like some of the followers of Jesus after his resurrection, they doubted (Matt. 28:17). They existed as a people because of God's miraculous deliverance, but they could not trust him for their daily bread. How can such a people announce his glory among the nations?

A People Is Born
But the decisive thing is that Israel has been brought out of Egypt, the movement has begun from the chaos of slavery to

a new life in God's land—the hope of a new creation has been raised. Little wonder this event becomes central in the imagination of Israel. It is remembered at special harvest festivals (Deut. 26:2-11), and eventually perhaps in special covenant renewal ceremonies such as that in Joshua 24. In these the event was not only recalled but made actual as Israel reconfirmed her faith.[6] The event marked the beginning of her history as a nation (1 Kings 6:1), and she celebrated it throughout the Psalter (cf. Ps. 78, 106 and 136).

But even in this deliverance God's universal purposes are hinted at. In Exodus 12:38 this unruly crowd is called a "mixed multitude," meaning probably that it not only included the actual descendants of Abraham but perhaps others anxious to leave the yoke of Pharaoh. From the beginning the way was always open for the foreigner to enjoy the blessings of Israel's God.

But of greatest significance remains the fact that here in a particular place God has acted to bring about salvation. Genesis (and our own experience) confirms that mankind has come into a situation in which they cannot save themselves. Something, someone must intervene or we are lost. Here then is an actual beginning of the historical shape of the kingdom into which God is calling all the nations. "There was initiated by the deliverance of Israel a historical movement which has not lost its force as a binding, community-forming and history-forming power until this day."[7] Notice, however, that not only does this event focus all of God's world-embracing promises, but the handing down of this account becomes a part of these purposes, a personal responsibility that is laid upon each Israelite family (Ex. 12:3-20). This witness points back to God's creation promises (Deut. 32:6) and ahead to future acts of God's deliverance—the central one of which Isaiah speaks of as a new exodus (Isa. 40—55).

But wherein lies the continuing relevance of the Exodus? Is it, as liberation theologians believe, a paradigm of God's will for all people? Gutierrez believes: "The Exodus experience is paradigmatic. It remains vital and contemporary due to similar historical experiences which the People of God undergo."[8] We can agree that the Exodus signifies God's intent to save people within the heart of history and not to take them out of history. And that salvation, since it deals with a real people in a concrete station, must involve a redistribution of power.[9]

While, in other words, Exodus points up God's desire to free slaves, its uniqueness lies in the fact that here in this instance of deliverance was actually begun a redemptive process that will prove determinative for the whole creative order and that will include in its purview the overthrow of all slavery. It is a redemptive symbol, but only because in the first instance it is an historical instance of redemption. Moreover, it belongs to God's covenant-making choice whereby a particular people become a vehicle of God's universal redemptive act in Jesus Christ. And it cannot be fully appreciated outside this biblical context.

A People Is Defined

It is clear by now that God desires to glorify himself in and through creation. This purpose is further defined by the fact that God is calling out a people that will reflect him by responding in obedience to his word. We have noticed furthermore that God seemed to make one covenant with creation, another with Noah, still another with Abraham and now another with the people at the Exodus. Much discussion has centered on the relation of these covenants to each other. Though there are obvious differences between them that relate to the historical situation in which they are made (God always meets his people where they are!), if we bear in mind God's overriding purpose to glorify himself we can see these covenants articulating a single program of God in creation. And while in every case he must take the initiative, there is always some response that is required that will embody his desires. One can say that each promise responds precisely to the need and potential of creation at that point and at the same time opens up a new dimension of responsibility for the people concerned (and eventually for the whole world through these representative figures). One does well then to see these covenants as progressive elaborations and expressions of God's redemptive rule (redemptive in that it must take account of and deal with human failure).

So just as the real significance of the Exodus event cannot be separated from the promise preceding it, it is also closely related to the giving of the law which follows. In the same way that the resurrection cannot be separated from the pouring out of the Holy Spirit in the New Testament, the act of calling his people out of slavery cannot be separated from the instructions which God now gives to assist them in regaining the dominion over creation they had lost at the fall. Sinai stands between the Exodus and the entrance into Canaan, as E. F. Campbell describes it, like a hinge of a great medieval diptych.[10]

Israel then is brought out of Egypt to "serve God upon the mountain" (Ex. 3:12). On the one hand, this means that the law always depends on this deliverance and reflects it at crucial points. Keeping the law was to be for Israel a form of remembering their deliverance (as verses like Exodus 23:9 and Deuteronomy 10:19 show). The law embodies a morality that reflects the character of deliverance. "Sinai is specific and demanding but its claim and its power are of the Exodus variety."[11]

The law, on the other hand, enables Israel to personally respond to God's covenant-making act in bringing them out of Egypt. As Genesis 15 records the enacted oath that binds the covenant God made with Abraham, so Exodus is the enacted oath that forms the basis for Israel's covenant relationship with her God. As they remembered the Exodus each Passover (Ex. 12), so in a higher sense we remember Christ's covenant-making death each time we take communion as his people. God who delivered Israel had a purpose for her that was to be the means of blessing the whole earth (Gen. 12:3), and this purpose was to be expressed and extended in their keeping of the law. Their response then was both the means of their knowing God and the way they would make him known to the world. To respond to God is to seek to reflect him in our concrete life. Incidentally the constant reiteration of "I am the Lord" throughout the law is probably a shortened way of emphasizing their calling to reflect him—imitate him as it were—in their treatment of each other and the land. For as John Murray puts it, the law is a "transcript of God's holiness."[12]

This way of thinking about the knowledge of God is so important that it demands special emphasis in this connection. Herbert Huffmon has pointed out that the usage of "to know" in Hebrew and related languages in the biblical period has taken on a technical meaning of "mutual legal recognition on the part of suzerain and vassal" and a "recognition of the treaty stipulations as binding."[13] So the references to God "knowing" Israel in the Pentateuch refer to the fact that he recognized them as his people by virtue of the covenant which he sealed with them at the Exodus. Israel for her part was to "know" (i.e., acknowledge) that God is the Lord (Deut. 4:35) by keeping the law which he has given (Ex. 31:13). Interestingly, though the prophets rarely mention the covenant, they often use the expression "know the Lord" in this technical sense, albeit with a new intimacy.

> He judged the cause of the poor and needy; then it was well. Is not this to know me? says the Lord. (Jer. 22:16; cf. 24:7; 31:34; and Amos 3:2, which someone has called Amos' theology of the covenant!)

This was the prophets' way of saying that Israel knew God by recognizing as binding the demands of the covenant expressed in the law. Incidentally the couplet "justice and righteousness" which appears so often may well be shorthand for social justice in general which God demands of his people (Gen. 18:19 and Amos 5:24).[14]

While this response called for the active obedience of his people, it was no less personal for that fact. It should be recalled in this connection that their obedience did not create the covenant; they were called to keep the law not in order to become God's people but because they already were by virtue of God's saving act. The purpose of the law then was to define the shape of this new life, to show them that all of life lay under the personal will of God (Deut. 6:5). This is why Moses could appeal in Deuteronomy (the so-called second giving of the law, which Moses gave just before their entrance into the land) for an inner personal acceptance of the law as the basis for just relations, health in the land and peace.[15] The fact that the law was an extension of God's promise to the Fathers "meant that the divine demand which was laid with such exclusive power on the individual, was from the beginning embedded in a history of this God with his people."[16] As we will note further on, the law too shows that God's purposes extend far into the texture of the social life of people in community and in history.

We have said that the character of the law itself reflects God's desire that his covenant people reflect him, and this point calls for special discussion here. It is true of course that in some respects the OT laws reflect a widespread customary law in the ancient Near East. Indeed, almost all of the Hebrew institutions have similarities with those of her neighbors. What God intended for Israel was not a people with unusual and unique customs, but a people—like all others in many ways—whose individual and corporate life reflected his character of justice and righteousness. To this end then God reveals the law to Moses, and so makes it a part of his redemptive and restorative purposes. That is, the law gives us an early indication of how God intends to bless Israel and make her a blessing to the nations. However similar to other laws, these laws display the essentially prophetic and witness-bearing nature of Israel's life. These are not laws for maintaining the status quo but rather have an impetus toward justice-making—especially in delivering the helpless—and the restoration of the created order. It is possible for us here to give only some examples of this from three areas of Israel's life.

Toward *persons* the law reflects a desire for the doing of justice and is specially worded to protect those who are in positions of helplessness (Deut. 10:17, 18; 15:7-11). During their nomadic existence all shared equally in God's provision. But God understood the way all economic and legal systems in a fallen world eventually work against those without power and resources; so provision is made in the law for the rights of the poor (Ex. 23:6). He knew the disadvantage at which foreign minorities were placed when they were abroad and so stipulated special care for them, reminding Israel, "you were strangers in the land of Egypt" (Ex. 23:9). Especially interesting is the treatment of the poor in the matter of a loan. The poor were not to pay interest and when they gave their coat as collateral, it was to be returned at nightfall (for "in what else shall he sleep?"—Ex. 22:25-27). Here the prophetic character of the law is seen, for while it recognizes the principle of collateral as legitimate, it protects those for whom the principle would work hardship.

In the case of slavery the law must have been subversive in its effect. Again the institution is not directly attacked, but the values of the slave as a person are consistently placed over property values. Hebrew slaves were to serve a maximum of six years and then be let free (with the additional command, "you shall furnish him liberally out of your flock"—Deut. 15:12-14). If they desired to stay on they could, but only because they declared their love for the master—love in this case is determinative of the legal relationship (Ex. 21:1-6). The sabbath legislation made special mention of the servants and slaves (even the animals!), for they too must have their rest (Deut. 5:14). Especially interesting is the instruction regarding harboring runaway slaves, which in the ancient Near East was usually a capital offense. In Deuteronomy, the runaway is not to be returned to his master (who presumably was mistreating him), but he is to settle down and pick a place to live among them "where it pleases him best" (23:15, 16). It is hard to imagine the institution of slavery surviving this injunction (which H. W. Wolff calls "unique in the ancient orient"[17]). Or rather the slavery that survived would be quite a different institution!

In the second place, toward *creation* instructions were given that encouraged restoration. The sabbath year provided for a time of rest for the land during which it could restore its fertility. What grew of itself was to be for the poor (Ex. 23:10, and Lev. 25:1-7). Every seventh sabbath year was a special jubilee year which was a kind of super-sabbath (see Lev. 25:8-55). On the day of atonement of the fiftieth year a trumpet was sounded, indicating that reconciliation with God was a prerequisite to reconciliation in human and creational relationships. The land was to be returned to its original heirs, indicating that finally God owns the land and Israel only held it in trust (25:23). Again slaves were released indicating that slavery at best was a temporary expedient and must eventually be abolished. And all debts were to be remitted, again providing assistance for those who, for one reason or another, had become impoverished. For "the dominance of the rich over the poor is a breach of God's covenant with the whole nation."[18] This more than anything else speaks of God's desire that structures exist that will correct the imbalance that enters into human relationships. In the prophets the jubilee came to be identified with the hope for a final settlement of rights and wrongs. Jubilee imagery is prominent especially in Isaiah, when the people had themselves become slaves in a foreign nation (Isa. 61:1, 2). These verses in fact became the text for Christ's first sermon in Nazareth in Luke 4:18-21 as he announces the purpose of his ministry. The jubilee idea then becomes an important precedent for the work of Christ.

But thirdly we mention the nature of the law to make *a place for Israel to meet with God*. In the weekly sabbaths (Ex. 23:12, 13), in the altars that God instructed them to build (Ex. 20:24), and finally in the various feasts (Lev. 23) Israel could remember their God and rejoice before him. Here the redemptive character of the law is clear. For God not only needed to instruct them in worship, but, from his side, he had to make provision for the atonement of their sins. Because of their sin they could not approach God any way they liked, but only when they had cleansed themselves and made themselves fit to stand in his presence. All these instructions climaxed on the day of atonement when a solemn offering was made for all the people and the blood was put on the goat who was then sent out into the wilderness (Lev. 16). The special place where God would meet with his people was the tent of meeting or the Tabernacle (Ex. 29:42-46), which was always to be erected in the midst of the camp. Interestingly in one of the first instances of the Spirit of God coming upon someone in the OT for a specific task, Bezalel is indwelt to make lovely designs for the Tabernacle (Ex. 31:1-5)! For there in the midst of the people was to be a special place of beauty and rest where God dwelt, reminding them every day of his kind purposes for their lives.

With the giving of the law, the shape of Israel's mission in the world begins to emerge. As Moses reminds the people in Deuteronomy, keeping the law was their "wisdom and understanding in the sight of the peoples. . . . For what great nation is there that has a god so near to it as the Lord our God is to us, whenever we call upon him? And what great nation is there, that has statutes and ordinances so righteous as all this law which I set before you this day?" (4:6-8). The purpose that God has in mind is that all the nations "know" (i.e., acknowledge) the Lord for themselves (Isa. 19:21), but the initial stage of this mission is to call one nation to know him. Note too that in the law the character of God's mission may be glimpsed for the first time. That is, God wills to show himself in Israel, so that the nations may come to Israel and eventually to Jerusalem to "see for themselves" his glory. In the OT the movement of the missionary thrust is primarily centripetal. The nations are invited to come up to Jerusalem (cf. Isa. 2:2-4). After the coming of Christ, however, the movement goes out from Jerusalem into the ends of the earth. Understanding the relationship between these two great world movements will be one of our primary goals in the pages to come.

Sadly Israel did not realize the heights to which it had been called, for while Moses was receiving the law from God, the people were down in the camp shaping and worshiping the golden calf.

Chapter Six

Entrance Into Canaan

Israel Learns Dependence in the Wilderness (Numbers)
The movement continues from Egypt to the land, and now the focus of the movement changes from deliverance to possession. Exodus 16—18 recounts the wilderness events which are elaborated in the book of Numbers, where, immediately following God's miraculous liberation, Israel is put to the test. For the land, though promised by God, must still be fought for (Num. 1:3); the people whom God has chosen as his firstborn must still learn obedience and trust.

The stage is set by the numbering of the men in preparation for war. More than 600,000 are counted (unless George Mendenhall's view is accepted that "thousand" means "tribe"), giving a total population of between two and three million. The family of Abraham has now grown to a considerable size, which implies that God has blessed it. But this same fact underlines the complete dependence of the people upon God's care, for where are provisions for such a crowd in the wilderness? But as if to prepare them for the trials that are to come, the first chapters of Numbers give particular signs of God's presence and care.

The first sign we mention is the famous benediction Aaron is instructed to pronounce over the people in 6:22-27. God here recalls the blessing at creation (Gen. 1:28) and the promised blessing through Abraham (Gen. 12:1-3) in a three-part blessing. First the Lord prospers and keeps in the "fundamental dimensions and requirements of human life."[1]

He will provide the basic assurance for life and provision. Second, the Lord makes his face to shine and is gracious— that is, he promises his presence in a personal way that provides deliverance and not the wrath that we deserve. And finally, the Lord lifts up his countenance and gives peace. Rest and peace speak in Scripture of the full and final supply for all that we lack, which God will one day give his people. Here a further dimension of Israel's mission is hinted: through the development of their understanding of God's presence and care they will be a vehicle of blessing. "The saving work of God in and through his people is a part of the blessing he bestows upon the world."[2]

The second sign of God's presence is the physical cloud and fire which is to lead them on their journey. This was to demonstrate to them God's command to leave or stay (Num. 9:15-23). Then special trumpets were to be made to gather the people "for a perpetual statute . . . that you may be remembered before the Lord your God, and you shall be saved from your enemies" (10:8, 9). The trumpet as a call to battle becomes an important symbol of the call to the final battle when Christ returns to judge the world (1 Cor. 15:52, and Rev. 8:2, 6). Already Israel must understand that as God gives the land, so he must fight for his people.

Finally in the eleventh chapter God appoints seventy leaders and endows them with some of the spirit of Moses to assist in administering the people. Immediately they begin to prophesy (vv. 24-27). When Joshua complains to Moses, Moses' answer comprises an interesting anticipation of God's will for his people: "Would that all the Lord's people were prophets, that the Lord would put his spirit upon them!" (v. 29). Clearly the narrator intends us to understand that this is a parallel gift to the giving of manna to eat (vv. 7-9). God's provision is both for the physical and social needs of his people and for their spiritual welfare; they need both the physical food and the word of God. As Moses expresses this in Deuteronomy 8:3:

And he humbled you and let you hunger and fed you with manna, which you did not know . . . that he might make you know that man does not live by bread alone, but that man lives by everything that proceeds out of the mouth of the Lord.

This verse Christ quoted when he was tempted in the wilderness to claim his own rights rather than trust in the provision and guidance of the Father. Christ may also have been thinking of the wilderness experience when he said, which one of you when your children ask for bread will give a serpent? If we give good gifts, "how much more will the heavenly Father give the Holy Spirit to those who ask him" (Luke 11:13).

But Israel was not satisfied either with the previous evidences of God's power, nor these present signs of his presence. Instead, as in Egypt, they cried out to the Lord. In fact, Walter Brueggemann has said of this period that the pattern of protest and answer becomes constitutive of the life of Israel.[3] God's glory continues to be shown in hearing the cries of his people and in making the empty full.

In spite of these assurances, as soon as they set out they complain about food, water and meat. God answers and gives them food and, as we saw, prophets who would give them the word of God. But in spite of their numbers and the presence of God in their midst, they tremble at the report of the spies (chap. 13) and do not believe the minority assurances of Joshua and Caleb. Because of their unbelief they are sentenced to wander for forty years so that only their children will see the land. Ironically it is the children—the little ones, who they feared would be prey to plunder—who will be allowed into the land (14:31). Truly the meek will inherit the earth, because they have only God to trust! Israel would "be victorious only when (God) purposes victory come."[4]

The wilderness experience was to become a fundamental part of Israel's self-consciousness, and constitutive for much of their worship in the Psalms. For the wilderness demanded surrender without security;[5] it required a minute by minute dependence upon God. The experience placed a total demand on them that is constantly recalled and that

Christ later picked up: will you leave all to follow the Lord?
(John 6:60-66). There too the disciples murmured at the
hard saying, and some no longer went around with Jesus.
But always there was the choice to be made: will you rebel
against God's rule, or will you trust?

> Fret not yourself; it tends only to evil.
> For the wicked shall be cut off;
> but those who wait for the Lord
> shall possess the land. (Ps. 37:8b, 9)

Israel Reflects on the Boundary of the Land (Deuteronomy)
In the final book of Moses Israel stands poised to take the
land. Just here at the delicate point between promise and
fulfillment, Israel is reminded of its unique mission. They
have already experienced the Exodus and Sinai; so they are
called on the one hand to remember what God has done
(7:17, 18). In fact, some of the nations of Canaan have
already been defeated (1:4), and God has blessed the
Israelites—multiplied them (1:10). Yet on the other hand
they are called to behold what God is about to do (20:4; cf.
Rev. 21:5). Gerhard von Rad has pointed out how much the
situation of Israel at this moment is like that of the NT
Church—standing between the already of redemption and
the not yet of possession.[6] Peter reiterates Moses' challenge
when he calls upon believers to "declare the wonderful
deeds of him who called you out of darkness" (1 Pet. 2:9).
And like Paul, Moses is urging Israel to become what God
has made them. Here "the outlines of the NT Christ-event
are . . . sketched in God's historical acts with Israel."[7]

  Significant too for our purposes is the role of Moses in
this book. Here he personally exhorts them to listen to God's
voice; he appeals to them on behalf of God as it were, as a
man to men, to respond to God's loving initiative. He reminds them that they now stand as recipients of God's blessing and that whatever happens in the future, they can always
return to "this day" and hear again God's word. For now
they stand in a unique relation to God (*Jahweh* and *your/our*

God appears 300 times in the book). On the one hand God has chosen them to be his special people, not because of their goodness, but because of his own righteousness and steadfast love (7:6-8). Here the holiness and sovereignty of God are to the fore. He is the single norm for his work with Israel. Yet on the other hand he is giving them this land, as at creation, to possess and have in dominion. It is a good land (this is repeated often in the book) with a great provision for their needs, though its goodness is pictured as a direct expression of God's grace (11:10-12)—so much so that it is anticipated that there will be no poor among them (15:4), if Israel is a faithful steward of its blessings. In short, it is a land in which God will give them rest from all their enemies (3:22; 12:10). Especially interesting is the call to remember God with their firstfruits in a special ceremony recalling God's guidance from the time of Abraham (26:1-10). Of course God does not need these gifts, but he invites Israel to bring them in token of the fact that all is his and he freely gives it. It is a reminder for them that the land is a place of giving—of God to them, they to God and to each other. The land is for sharing.

But the land will not only be a blessing; it will also be a challenge. In that strange expression God reminds them that he has given them the land to possess (5:31; 6:1; 12:1; et al). While the land is totally a gift, it will also be completely Israel's responsibility. Constantly God reminds them of the statutes he has given them for the land (4:5, 14; 5:31).[8] In fact the entire central section of the book (chapters 12—26) is given over to a second exposition of the law. So while Deuteronomy is about a gift, it also contains law. "It is gospel and then law—both completely intertwined, inextricable one from the other. There is no such thing in the concept of Torah as law without story."[9] The link between these two is to be found in 8:10-18. When you are satisfied, Moses warns them, bless the Lord for the good land he has given you, for (v. 18) it is God "who gives you the ability to produce wealth and so confirms his covenant" (NIV). Though their response is necessary to the fulfillment of the covenant, this too is given by God.

Israel is never to think her righteousness provides the grounds for God's goodness. Quite the contrary: Moses has to remind them that they are a stiff-necked people (9:6, 7). The other side of God's giving of the land is that the Canaanites have to be driven out. Israel's blessing is accompanied by their judgment. But this too can be understood as a test between their gods and Israel's. Clearly it is "because of the wickedness of these nations the Lord your God is driving them out from before you" (9:5), and so he can confirm his covenant to the Fathers. Once again it is for his sake that he saves Israel and, through Israel, the nations.

Moses then has to remind them of the threats to their obedience that will exist in the land. There will be diviners and idolatry associated with the heathen cults (chap. 13); there will be a generation gap between those brought into the land and those raised there (11:2; 6:20-24); then there will be the familiar faintheartedness before these strange peoples (7:17). But these threats all belong to the temptation not to remember who God had showed himself to be. It is up to them to choose blessing or a curse (11:26).

And what is the significance of the choice that Israel will make? Is it a local matter between a local God and his people? This point is dramatically dealt with in chapters 27—30. For there will be consequences to their response, and these consequences are not limited to Israel. History and nature are open to God's direction, and this rule is directly related to Israel's obedience or disobedience. For the fate of the nations, indeed of heaven and earth, is now tied to the people that God has chosen for his own. Foreigners will come and ask why the land is barren. Then the answer will come: "It is because they forsook the covenant of the Lord" (29:24, 25). This is why in 30:19 Moses calls heaven and earth to witness the life and death decision he sets before them. Once again the whole creation waits to see the response of Israel.

That the fate of the nations is linked to that of Israel is hinted at in two further enigmatic verses. In 32:43 the nations are invited to praise God's people, "for he avenges the blood of his servants and takes vengeance on his adversaries." Then 33:29 notes that Israel is happy as a people saved by the Lord: "Your enemies shall come fawning to you; and you shall tread upon their high places." The peoples of the earth are to look to Israel and her land as a place of salvation, and yet, in some way not yet clear, that place will mean judgment for them.

God Takes the Land and Gives It to Israel (Joshua)

The book of Joshua continues all the major themes of Deuteronomy—the covenant and the law, the holy war and the call to obedience in the land. But now the time of fulfillment approaches; Israel is coming into the land which God has promised her. Once again the responsibility of Israel is underlined: though God gives the land, it will have to be fought for. However, just as he has given the land, so he will fight for Israel. His "overthrow of the enemy is the way they and the land are given over to Israel."[10]

The fact that God himself has made use of war as an instrument of his providence—as we might even say, a means of his mission—is so prominent and so troublesome that we must reflect further on it. How can God use war as a means to peace? The imagery of battle is of course central in Scripture from the very beginning. Later reflections on creation picture it as a great battle with the forces of chaos (Ps. 89). And in Genesis 3:15 as a part of the curse we recall that an enmity has been placed between the seed of the woman and that of the serpent. Thus at the inception of God's redemptive program there is implied an impending struggle between God and the powers of evil, a battle in which there will be casualties on both sides, but which will finally be decided in favor of the seed of the woman. Then the rescue from Egypt is pictured as a great battle, and for the first time God is clearly called a "man of war" (Ex. 15:3) who has triumphed gloriously. The battle theme is continued in the NT where the ministry of Christ is pictured as a struggle against the powers of evil, over which Christ conquers with his death and resurrection (Col. 2:15). Though the decisive battle has been won, the Christian now carries on a continual skirmish against evil (2 Cor. 10:4, 5) which anticipates the great climactic battle of Revelation 19.

So the wars of Canaan must be understood as a part of God's struggle with the forces of evil. But these have a unique character that scholars call the holy war. In the first place God declares these wars and gives them their sanction (Deut. 20:4). The commander holds his office because the Spirit of the Lord comes upon him (Judg. 6:34). Those who fight the battle must keep themselves ceremonially clean (recall Uriah's refusal to go in to Bathsheba when on leave), and no fainthearted or preoccupied soldiers are allowed into the battle (Deut. 20:5-9). These wars then are "a responsibility under the covenant, and cultically as a sacrificial act, initiated by the will of Yahweh and carried out by people devoted to his service and ceremonially pure."[11]

Holy wars were determined at a particular point in history for a purpose. They must be understood in terms of God's righteousness (his deliverances in Canaan are called in fact "righteous acts"—cf. Judg. 5:11 in Hebrew) and his judgment upon evil. We noticed before how his deliverance always has the double character of judgment upon evil and the salvation of his people. Thus the other side of God's merciful giving of the land to Israel is that it must be taken from the Canaanites who, because of their wickedness (which included child sacrifice), have brought upon themselves the righteous wrath of God. There is indication moreover that those upon whom God visits his judgment have brought this about because their iniquity is complete (see Gen. 15:16).

On the other hand, Israel was a small undeveloped nation in the midst of a grossly pagan people. John Wenham comments: "For centuries on end the very survival of the cause of true religion seemed to hang on a thread."[12] An underlying theme then is the struggle with the powers of evil and the false gods of Canaan. When the Philistines capture the ark, they assume that their god, Dagon, is greater than the God of Israel (Judg. 16:23 and 1 Sam. 5). The so-called ban, or complete destruction of cities and their inhabitants, must also be understood in this context. These cities have become, because of their wickedness, devoted to destruction and so the entire city becomes a sacrifice to God (Josh. 6:17).

So wars become an instrument by which eventually God will cause all wars to cease (Ps. 46:8, 9) and by which he brings his people into possession of the land and gives them rest from all their enemies. But Israel had to remember that though the battle was the Lord's (1 Sam. 17:47), it could be lost because of their sin (as happened in the case of Achan in Josh. 7:1-5, 15-26). And things could come to such a state that, in the prophets, God is seen to fight against his people!

While the first half of Joshua is given over to the conquest of the land under Joshua (climaxing in the list of defeated kings in chapter 12), the rest describes the division of the land among the people. God has (re)taken the land and Israel is given rest from all her enemies (21:44, 45). Now Israel, his firstborn, is made to "inherit" the land and to pass it on to their heirs. It becomes a trust which they must tend and nurture, just as Adam and Eve were called to do in the garden of Eden. As in the beginning too there is plenty to provide for all of Israel; each tribe has its own portion. Here again is sounded the vital theme of the interrelationship of people, nature and history which continues to highlight God's redemptive program. "The idea of inheritance," writes Walter Brueggemann, "affirms that there are enduring and resilient networks of meaning and relationship into which one is placed, and these are fundamental to the shape of society."[13] But that means Israel is confronted with a great challenge, which Joshua outlines in Joshua 23 and 24 (in what may be an example of a yearly covenant renewal ceremony). They must choose to fear God and serve him, for if they turn away and serve the gods of the Canaanites, God will cause them to "perish quickly from off the good land" which he had given them (23:16).

God's People Possess the Land (Judges)
Judges begins with fulfillment and ends in despair. Chapter

1 recounts victories in the land and even the taking of Jerusalem, but adds solemnly that they "did not drive out the Canaanites" (vv. 27, 29, 30, 31, 33). Chapter 2 returns to the time of Joshua's death and notes that no sooner have they taken over their inheritance than they begin to serve other gods (v. 13). At that time God begins to raise up judges to "save them out of the power of those who plundered them" (v. 16), but Israel does not listen to them (v. 17), and so God delivers them into the hand of their enemies (3:8).

Now the familiar pattern is repeated. Israel is oppressed and they cry out to the Lord, so the Lord sends a deliverer (3:15; 4:3, 4). Finally God sends Deborah, decisive victories are won and the northern and central groups of tribes are united. These victories are celebrated in the ancient Song of Deborah in chapter 5. Like Exodus 15 before it, this recounts the triumphs of the Lord in terms of a cosmic battle with the forces of evil and chaos (vv. 4, 5) and recalls Israel's covenant obligation as a summons to common action. The chapter ends by noting: "The land had rest for forty years" (v. 31). God's purposes have triumphed in spite of the unfaithfulness of his people; he has raised up a deliverer.

The office of judge is of particular importance in the history of God's messengers. The judges' primary purpose is to deliver Israel from the hand of her enemies by leading the Israelites in battle (2:16). But they are also to judge the people wisely (4:4, 5). Especially interesting is the example of Gideon, for after his victories the people seek to make him king. He responds: "I will not rule over you, and my son will not rule over you; the Lord will rule over you" (8:23). Thus he shows that the true judge rules in God's stead and at his word.

But Israel would not listen. Immediately following the paean of the Song of Deborah, 6:1 begins: "The people of Israel did what was evil in the sight of the Lord." When finally all seems lost, 13:1 says that God gave Israel into the hands of their enemies for forty years. But just at this point a son is promised to a barren woman (13:3) and our hearts quicken: a seed! He is set apart for God and the Spirit of the Lord is upon him (13:25). But what a strange deliverer Samson turns out to be! James Wharton comments: "Jahweh is underway in the world to free his people from Philistine tyranny, though not a soul in the story knows it and his chosen instrument looks very like an oversexed buffoon."[14] Just when things seem blackest and even God's deliverer fails, precisely at his moment of humiliation there is deliverance. For Samson slew more Philistines at his death than during his lifetime (16:30). So God shows himself Lord over the gods of the Philistines.

But there seems no one to celebrate this great victory; they are too busy quarreling over their inheritance and making merry with the Canaanites. Things seem to come to a new low when the book ends: "In those days there was no king in Israel; every man did what was right in his own eyes" (21:25). Once again the good thing that God has promised seems to be hopelessly lost and Israel's faith is sorely tested. What, we wonder, can be the meaning of this promised land? What has become of God's promises? It can be no accident that just at this point, chronologically, appears the marvelous Book of Ruth. For if God's own people have no vision for what God intends, here is a foreign woman who sees more clearly: "Your people shall be my people, and your God my God" (1:16). Through her, God will bring a son, David, who will rule in token of his greater son, the Lord Jesus. Here too the land figures prominently, for though Elimelech and Naomi have to travel to Moab because of a famine in the land, Naomi and Ruth return when "the Lord had visited his people and given them food" (1:6), and there the Lord raises up seed to Elimelech, who had died in Moab. So God's rule advances, a people are forming, and the land is theirs. This rule can of course be withstood; but it cannot be overthrown. And Ruth the Moabitess is a sign that the blessings of it are for the whole world.

Before we leave our discussion of the land, two issues call for comment. We are used to thinking of God's use of the land in the OT as a kind of object lesson of spiritual truths that he wishes to communicate. Surely, we say, actual land cannot figure in God's program of salvation. But to draw this conclusion is to overlook the biblical context of creation (and the new creation) in which salvation is set. Salvation can no more be separated from the land (or the total created context) than people can be abstracted from their bodily and social existence. The meaning of Israel's possession of the land is not so much an object lesson as a token of what God intends for all his creation. As he began with one man to reach the world, so he begins with one land to renew the whole; and the one program cannot be separated from the other. God brought Israel into the land to set their feet in an open place (Ps. 66:12), which is to say in biblical terminology, he made them enjoy salvation. Though rich in promise of what God intended to do later, we should be careful not to look on the salvation that God gave his people in the OT as only the promise of good things. As the Psalms so amply show, the Hebrews enjoyed real salvation, not just the hope of deliverance (see Psa. 19, 20, 68 *et al*). For though progressive and cumulative, God's purposes were never insufficient at the point they were revealed.

What then can we say about the character of salvation to this point? We have noted that it includes both judgment and deliverance within its purview. For God's people "deliverance is imparted to the weak in virtue of a relation of protection or dependence in which he stands to someone stronger or mightier who saves him out of his affliction."[15] This involves the fully personal appeal or cry of God's people and his response in remembrance of the promises to the Fathers. Second, this deliverance is embodied in specific events in which God intervenes and saves his people in their helplessness. Since his saving acts are for his name's sake and in spite of the sins of his people, the forensic element must always be present. There must be the atonement, or passing over, of sin through the payment of a gift or offering (cf. the passover and Ex. 34:20). Finally God's deliverance includes material supply and provision for the renewal of the created order. The wilderness theme of "lacking nothing" and the bounty of the land into which God was bringing them must certainly be included in the salvation idea as the OT reveals it. Salvation then carries over the fundamental provision of creation and accompanies it with God's merciful and delivering presence. These elements will of course be enriched in the course of Scripture; it is hard to see how any could be eliminated.

The second comment relates directly to the land and God's missionary purposes. Canaan will now, and to the end of time, be the special arena for the kingdom of God. In short, we can say that Israel is brought into the land so that the nations may behold God's glory. Canaan after all can hardly be called a destination in any sense of the word; it is more of a crossroads. It is a place where Israel will lie in wait for the nations, for sooner or later all peoples must pass this way. As Jerusalem becomes more and more the focus of attention, we will notice that though it becomes central in God's program, it is never meant to be a retreat. One can almost say that it will be Israel's mission to stick in the craw of the nations, to be a pointer and a vehicle of something they often barely perceived: the rule of God.

So both the purposes of God and the failure of his people decreed that possession of the land was not the final goal of the promises to Abraham. It is a decisive fulfillment, but at the same time a token of something better. For God always points his people ahead, and the further one moves through Scripture the broader the horizon of the future becomes.

Chapter Seven

The Monarchy

Who Rules over Israel?

Though God is rarely called king, his right to reign over his people is established by his mighty deliverance from Egypt; the Song of Moses concludes: "The Lord will reign for ever and ever" (Ex. 15:18). In the OT, however, this rule was mediated through people especially called to govern. In fact, from the beginning there is an intimation that the blessing of God promised to the nations will come through kings. Abraham is promised that kings will come from him (Gen. 17:6); Judah is promised the scepter "until he comes to whom it belongs" (Gen. 49:10), which continues "and to him shall be the obedience of the peoples." Then Balaam's oracle envisions a scepter rising from Israel who will crush the forehead of Moab (Num. 24:17). So just as he promised a prophet to come after Moses, God promised his people a king, but one that he would give them in his own time. From the beginning the idea is present that through God's king the nations of the earth will be judged, a judgment here portrayed under the imagery of military conquest.

The programmatic statements for both the office of the king and the prophet appear in Deuteronomy 17 and 18. The prophet we will consider later, but let it be noted here that in both descriptions Moses refers both to an office and an ideal type. The human king introduced in Deuteronomy 17:14-20 reigns as a special reflection of God's own rule. As

H. W. Wolff points out, the unique glory of Israel was its origin as a group of slaves delivered from Egypt.[1] Kingship when it came about must always reflect the character of this peculiar people who God had called out of darkness. So the law of the king of Deuteronomy 17 is unique in the ancient Near East.

First the king is to be one whom the Lord chooses; his role as the anointed of God is primary. Then he is to be from among their brethren (v. 15); that is, he is to rule as a brother among brothers, not as a god descended from a divine pantheon. He must not multiply possessions or wives, which in the ancient Near East are primary signs of wealth and prestige. Finally, he must write the law for himself (has the king no scribe?) and "learn to fear the Lord his God, by keeping all the words of this law . . . that his heart may not be lifted up above his brethren" (vv. 19, 20). As in the case of slavery, here is a law that is subversive of the institution of kingship as it existed in the Near East. He is to do none of the things that kings always do—flaunt their wealth and power—and rule as no king had ever dreamed of ruling—by serving the law. As the king was to reflect God's own merciful rule among his people and speak of a ruler who was to come, we will notice that the office of king becomes the special arena of struggle with the powers of evil.

This struggle is apparent in the long-standing antipathy toward kingship that existed in Israel and that expressed itself in Gideon's refusal to rule and in Jotham's parable (Judg. 9:15): God is our ruler and if we insist on a human king in our insecurity we shall have exactly the ruler we deserve. There is something prophetic about this, for it is the crisis situation of the early chapters of 1 Samuel that causes Israel to cry out for a king. In 1 Samuel 4, 30,000 fall at the hands of the Philistines and the ark is captured, but because of their repentance (they cry to the Lord, 7:8) they win a great victory at Mizpah and the Lord is with Israel all the days of Samuel's life. But still they want a king "like all the nations" (8:5). Israel, who is to be a blessing to the nations, wants now only to ape them! Dennis McCarthy in his study of these chapters[2] has shown how the narration of the story here points up the basic tensions in attitudes toward kingship: is it given or grasped? Is it a fulfillment or violation of God's promises? In the eighth chapter of 1 Samuel it appears evil because it seeks what only God can give (vv. 8, 20). Still, in chapter 9 Saul is introduced positively as one who will save his people (v. 16), though in chapter 10 problems arise (vv. 17-19, 25-27). But lo and behold, in 13:1-3 Saul acts like God's man! Surely they can rejoice in their king; but, wait a minute, Samuel speaks again in chapter 12 and recalls the problems of chapter 8. Finally 12:13 gives a new call to obedience, "all the people greatly feared the Lord" (v. 18), and the covenant is renewed (vv. 22-24). Now, notes McCarthy, "a new era can begin,"[3] and kingship becomes a part of God's purposes for his people.

God Has a King for His People

As we have implied, it was not only God's intention to concede to Israel's desire for a king; he had it in mind to rule them through a king from the beginning and to incorporate kingship into his covenant promises. But it was to be a particular kind of king. Let us look at the relevant passages which outline the kingship that God had in mind for his people. The classic passage is the promise given through Nathan in 2 Samuel 7. The context is full of promise for Israel. Verse 1 tells us that the king was dwelling securely in his house because the Lord had given him rest from all his enemies (remember how important rest is as a sign of God's blessing). David then reflects upon the fact that while he has a place to dwell, God is still dwelling in a tent; so he informs Nathan that he will build God a house. The response that God gives to Nathan during that night is very interesting. It implies that David has it all wrong in wanting a house for him (did I ever ask anyone to build me a house?—v. 7). It is not David who will build a house for God, but God who intends to build David a house (vv. 8-13). "I will give him a son (seed!), whose throne I will establish forever." Note that

he will be a son to God and God will be his Father (v. 14);
though God will punish him, he will not remove his steadfast
love from him.

This promise, usually called the Davidic covenant, is
not really a new covenant so much as a means by which the
covenant to Abraham—renewed and extended—will be established. Often a sharp distinction is made between the
promises to Moses and those to David; the former seem to
be conditional upon Israel's response (Ex. 19:5), the latter
are unconditional in emphasis (2 Sam. 7:15). While it is true
that during the prophets these developed into traditions that
opposed one another,[4] and the promise to David seems to
lack the former stipulations (though cf. 1 Kings 9:4), we
prefer to see the later covenant as an elaboration of the basic
promises to Abraham and Moses (both of which also stress
the unconditional aspect of God's election—see Gen. 17:7
and Deut. 7:6-10). As Dennis McCarthy puts it, the "Davidic covenant continues and specifies the older one."[5] After all,
God originally wanted a relationship of sonship with all
Israel (Ex. 4:22). This particular son, then, will be the means
of facilitating the sonship of all.

This intimation is made even clearer in the enthrone-
ment ceremonies which developed in Israel (cf. 1 Kings 1
and 2 Kings 11) and which are probably reflected in various
Psalms. Psalm 2, for example, pictures the earthly enthrone-
ment of the king as his adoption by God:

> He said to me: "You are my son, today I have begotten you."
> (2:7)

Verse 8 goes on to say that God intends to give this king the
nations as his inheritance and the ends of the earth as his
possession. This recalls the promise of dominion to Adam
and Eve and also the promise to Abraham. But once again
the relationship to the nations will issue in their judgment
(v. 9).

But like the first dominion-haver, this king is to reflect
God by the character of his ruling, as we have seen in

Deuteronomy 17. This is made clear in Psalm 72, which interestingly is called a Psalm of Solomon. The king is to be given God's own justice (v. 1), which will result in prosperity in the mountains and hills (v. 3) and also in his defense of the cause of the poor (v. 4). In the Deuteronomy passage the particular character of Israel as a delivered slave people is recalled and the unique nature of the law—which the king is to read and remember—is underlined. A king then is to rule as a servant and exhibit in a higher way that fundamental ministry-character of human life which we noted in the creation account. In a fallen world this ministry will mean caring for those unable to care for themselves, those in need of deliverance. Such a king will have dominion from sea to sea, and, note well, the kings of Tarshish and the isles will come and render him tribute (Ps. 72:10, 11). Even allowing for oriental hyperbole, John Bright is certainly correct when he observes that this prayer "seems to outrun all reality."[6] Tarshish was in Spain (or perhaps Sardinia), at the outer limits of the then known world. How can any earthly king (of a second-rate power!) deserve such honor? As if in answer to this question, the Psalm goes on to reiterate the mark of the rule of God's king:

> For he delivers the needy when he calls,
> the poor and him who has no helper.
> He has pity on the weak and the needy,
> and saves the lives of the needy.
> From oppression and violence he
> redeems their lives. (vv. 12-14)

Such a Godlike rule will endure and the earth will prosper under his reign (v. 16).

These themes are sounded also in Psalms 89 and 110. In the former the parallel with 2 Samuel is clear. The promise of Nathan is repeated and elaborated and climaxes in verse 27: "And I will make him the firstborn, the highest of the kings of the earth." Psalm 110 speaks of David ruling until all his enemies are subdued—until, that is, dominion and righteousness are restored to the earth. Though in a world that is evil, righteous dominion must somehow involve judgment for the nations (vv. 5, 6).

These promises must have thrilled the worshipers at the Temple as they gathered to crown their kings. Indeed they issued in a tradition featuring the Davidic throne and God's presence in Zion that influenced Jewish thinking up until NT times. And when Solomon (David's son!) is crowned in splendor in Jerusalem, when the ark (the throne of God!) is brought into the Temple in 1 Kings 8, Israel could be forgiven for thinking that these hopes were being fulfilled before their eyes. Surely Jerusalem, the throne of God's king (and of God himself), was becoming a place to which all the nations would look (see Ps. 48:1, 2). S. Talmon observes of this era, "Mt. Zion and the covenant that God established there with David, represent Israel's sovereignty in its full bloom, in civil and sacred life."[7]

But Is This Really the Kingdom That God Promised?

Is it really possible for an earthly king to reflect God? Was not the monarchy more of a disaster to Israel than a blessing? One does not have to read far in the book of the kings to ask such questions. Scholars writing recently about the kings have gone to great lengths to underline the negative influence of the monarchy on the life of Israel.[8]

Consider the fact that kingship in the first instance was established as a political expedient. As we have seen, the early chapters of 1 Samuel picture the grim situation Israel faced in trying to subdue her enemies. Thus Israel first sought a king because she did not trust God to deliver her. Her idea of a king resulted not from his special ministry among them, but from their insecurity and the desire to be like all the other nations.

Then there is the obviously foreign character of the Jerusalem monarchy. George Mendenhall goes so far as to say that "virtually every cultural aspect of the Jerusalem regime is derived from the very complex merging of . . . cultural traditions of the Bronze Age, except for some few features derived from Egypt."[9] Seen in this light, the Temple itself is not so much a unique testimonial to Jahweh as a "monument to Hittite architectural traditions."[10] Like the kingship, it existed because other people had such a temple to their gods, and Israel did not want to seem out of place among her neighbors. Brueggemann concludes that its whole function was "to give theological legitimacy to the entire program of the regime."[11] God does not act there, he notes wryly, he abides!

Key personnel in David's administration are also foreign. Even Zadok his priest is probably of Canaanite origin. The very word "Zion," Mendenhall notes, betrays Hittite origin.[12] What became of the ancient wilderness traditions?

Worst of all, the whole process of urbanization seemed to involve a progressive loss of ethical and spiritual sensitivity. The rise of a monetary economy may lie at the root of abuses singled out by the prophets. David probably took over existing administrative centers, and inevitably economic and political matters took priority over ancient traditions (can these meet the demands of the "modern" world after all?). Customary law gave way to state-supported legal systems. Forced labor became the rule under Solomon. We have come a long way from Egypt! H. W. Wolff concludes: "Thus the area ruled by the successors of David was reduced precisely because Israel's free men had been enslaved."[13] In only two generations of evolution of the Jerusalem kingship, Mendenhall points out, we have a reversion to Bronze Age paganism.[14]

There is, of course, a great deal of truth in these allegations, and there were not wanting prophets steeped in the ancient traditions who took such a line. Some think that Adonijah was such a prophet; later Hosea reflected a northern rural tradition that had always been suspicious of the monarchy. But not everything recorded in Kings fits such a construction. While the kings are forbidden from entering into foreign alliances, there is never any indication that all foreign borrowing was wrong. After all, Israel had been a seminomadic people and had no traditions of administration

and kingship of her own. The law of the king in Deuteronomy 17, like the other laws we reviewed, was not given to
specify an institution different from their neighbors, but to
lend the same institution a wholly different character. Moreover, to emphasize the foreign origin of people and words is
to commit the genetic fallacy: the view that the origin of
something determines its character. But this was certainly
not the case with Ruth, or the furnishings of the Tabernacle
which God himself specified. Foreign influence had been
constant in Israel; indeed, as we pointed out, Israel is put in
a land where she cannot avoid, is not meant to avoid borrowing. For God intended even these administrative and com-
mercial structures to reflect his loving justice. All these
things were capable of being taken up into God's program of
redemption which decrees finally that all the glory of the
nations should be brought into Jerusalem (Rev. 21:24).

The point is that with the monarchy Israel has taken its
place in the history of the nations, it has been inserted into a
world history that henceforth can never be the same. True,
Israel (and Judah) soon forgot the covenant traditions, and
paganism began to infiltrate their institutions. The prophets
that soon announce their message from God did not con-
demn her institutions as such, but rather what Israel had
done to them.[15] The real question is: what did God intend to
accomplish through the monarchy, and is there any indication that he was successful in this? We have noted already
some of his purposes, and we will presently inquire into
their success. The real problem, as Eichrodt points out, is
the problem of sin. As the early chapters of Genesis show its
infiltration into every corner of public life, so the monarchy
is commissioned to construct a rule that would reflect righteousness. (Brueggemann[16] in fact believes the final version
of Genesis 1—11 was edited during the height of the monarchy to warn it of the consequences of unfaithfulness.) But
soon the sad reality became evident: "There is no end to the
attempt to make the monarchy an exception to the duty of
obedience to the divine command."[17]

The strongest evidence for the fact that God's purposes

were not frustrated in the monarchy, however, is that there were kings who did reflect his ideal. David and Solomon extended and secured the land promised to Abraham. Asa did what was right in the sight of God (1 Kings 15:9-24); Hezekiah, after his illness, brought about a reform in Judah; and Josiah set in motion a far-reaching return to the covenant demands. None of these perfectly reflected God's promised king, but they pointed in that direction, and God used even their imperfect examples as witnesses to his purposes.

This becomes clearer when we take a closer look at the case of Solomon. As in 1 Samuel 8—12 which we studied above, the record of Solomon's reign contains a similar tension: was Solomon a fulfillment of God's promises to David or a betrayal of them? A clear answer is not forthcoming. (We would, of course, find the same ambiguities present in the life of David.[18]) Take the matter of the Temple. Several chapters are given over to the building of the great structure where God was to dwell and to Solomon's prayer of dedication (1 Kings 6—9). Solomon's prayer is impressive; surely here is a king who understands and reveres the ancient traditions. But to build the Temple Solomon used a forced levy of slaves (9:21, 22); while he took seven years to build the Temple, he took thirteen years to build his own house (6:37, 38 and 7:1)! Is this really the house that God wants? Whatever its weaknesses, however, God answers Solomon's prayer, and promises:

> I have consecrated this house which you have built, and put my name there for ever; my eyes and my heart will be there for all time. (1 Kings 9:3)

But as if to emphasize his overriding concern he goes on immediately to reiterate the promise to David: if he keeps God's statutes, his throne will be eternal. Clearly God has accepted the Temple and taken it up into his re-creative program. It becomes the symbol of perfect restoration in Ezekiel. In the ministry of Jesus (especially in John) it be-

comes a symbol of God's purpose of communion with his
people, which is fulfilled in the work of Christ and revealed
in the ministry of the Holy Spirit, who dwells in our bodies
as his own temple (1 Cor. 6:19).

But is Solomon himself the king that God predicted
would reign as David's son? Before we are quick to dismiss
such a notion we need to reread these chapters. In 1 Kings 3
Solomon asks God for wisdom to rule his people righteously—that is, to have the dominion God desires. And God
gives him what he requests (1 Kings 3:11-14), and his great
wisdom becomes known all over the world. Then 1 Kings
4:20, 21 makes the astounding claim:

> Judah and Israel were as many as the sand by the sea; they
> ate and drank and were happy. Solomon ruled over all the
> kingdoms from the Euphrates to the land of the Philistines
> and to the border of Egypt; they brought tribute and served
> Solomon all the days of his life.

The narrator wants us to understand that Solomon has plainly fulfilled the promises of God to Abraham in Genesis 22:17
and 15:18 respectively. Beyond that, the honor of the nations which Psalm 2:8 spoke of has already begun. This final
claim brings us to the climax of the incidents associated with
the reign of Solomon. In his prayer Solomon had spoken of
foreigners who would hear of God's great name and would
pray toward the Temple. Solomon asks God to hear them "in
order that all the peoples of the earth may know thy name
and fear thee" (1 Kings 8:43). Before long these hints take
flesh in the form of the visit of the Queen of Sheba with her
great retinue of camels laden with gifts (1 Kings 10). When
she saw all that Solomon had done, she was breathless. She
told him, "Blessed be the Lord your God, who has delighted
in you and set you on the throne of Israel! Because the Lord
loved Israel for ever, he has made you king, that you may
execute justice and righteousness" (10:9).

Here are events rich in promise. While there is as yet
no active faith or clear view of Israel's relation to the nations,

there is already a sense, as H. Rowley put it, of the infinite treasure entrusted to Israel.[19] And there is also the first sign of the journey of the Gentiles toward Jerusalem, a pilgrimage the prophets hint will one day include all the peoples of the earth. The first concrete evidence of God's mission to the world has appeared.

While all this enables us to see in Solomon evidence of God's purposes for the king, the narrator leaves us under no illusion as to Solomon's real character. He makes alliances with Pharaoh (1 Kings 3:1) and Hiram (5:12); he imperiously gives away portions of the land (which God had entrusted to him—9:11-14); he uses forced labor in building the Temple (9:20, 21); he loved many foreign women, had many wives and great herds of horses and chariots (11:1-9; 10:26-28). All the things proscribed in the covenant and the law of the king, Solomon does. The kings that follow him, with unbroken monotony, follow also (with the exceptions we have noted) in his ways, and the litany is repeated; they do what is evil in the sight of God, until the inevitable yet incredible end. Second Kings 17 records the exile of the northern state and 2 Kings 24 that of the south. First and 2 Chronicles equate David's throne with God's throne, and show that it was God's desire that his promise to David carry out his loving purposes in these new political and economic dimensions. But as in the wilderness and in the period of the judges, here too Israel failed to fulfill her calling. Whether out of frustration or anger, there must have been many who wondered, where is the king who will rule in righteousness?

The Witness of Wisdom

Because part of Solomon's credentials as "David's better son" consist in his special gift of wisdom, it would not be out of place for us to comment here on the contribution of the wisdom movement in the OT. The wisdom literature in the Bible—Job, certain Psalms, Proverbs and Ecclesiastes—reflects the influence of the widespread wisdom movement in the ancient Near East, whose origins lie well back in the third millennium B.C. In Israel's history it is identified with a specially trained group of people, perhaps from the upper classes,[20] which during the monarchy took definite shape and had wide influence on the life of Israel, even upon the prophets.

Wisdom consisted basically in the art of "steering" or getting along in life (Prov. 1:5) and, as Solomon illustrated, included broad knowledge as well as astute statesmanship (1 Kings 4:29-34). The prominence of "nature wisdom" in this account—"He spoke of trees . . . of beasts, and of birds and of reptiles, and of fish" (v. 33)—points up the close relation between creation and wisdom. The wise person is the one heading in the direction of having dominion over creation (Gen. 1:28). Moreover, it illustrates that there is a moral order implanted in creation by which righteousness issues in a solid and healthy life. The person exists in a responsible relationship to this order and its demands. Wealth is a blessing, but there is something higher: the knowledge or fear of God, which is the beginning of true wisdom (Prov. 1:7). The wise person is one who knows the limitation of human wisdom (16:25) and acknowledges the direction that comes from God (3:5-7). Here then is yet another case of God's taking up into his redemptive program the glory of the nations: Joseph can shine among the wise in Egypt, Moses' strength can confuse the magicians of Pharaoh, and Daniel and his friends could prosper above all the wise of Babylon. There is no biblical case for anti-intellectualism as a mark of the believer. To the contrary, the faith of God's people could be made to shine in this setting so that the Queen of Sheba could come and give glory to God.

But there is something more important here. Proverbs presents wisdom as calling out to people (Prov. 1:20-23), and chapter 8 pictures wisdom forming the very rationality of creation as though it were almost human. At the close of this great passage, in fact, wisdom takes voice and urges:

Now, my sons, listen to me:
Happy are those who keep my ways. . . .

Happy is the man who listens to me,
    watching daily at my gates,
    waiting beside my doors.
For he who finds me finds life
And obtains favor from the Lord.
                    (vv. 32, 34, 35)

What is there in this world that can make such a personal appeal? Scholars agree that it is better to see this as a poetic personification rather than any literal hypostatization. But as Derek Kidner has put it, we know from Colossians 1:15-20 "that the personifying of wisdom, far from overshooting the literal truth, was a preparation for its full statement."[21] For it was precisely the mission of Jesus the God-man, who John tells us is the *logos* or order of creation, to call us personally to come to him and find life (John 14:6). Paul takes this line of thinking a step further in 1 Corinthians 1. Contrary to what most observers think, Paul says, the Jesus Christ that we preach is not foolishness but the very wisdom of God and of creation—"to those who are called, both Jews and Greeks, Christ the power of God and the wisdom of God" (v. 24). Thus our gospel message is not an isolated story, but is rooted in the very order of things and inserts people into God's fullest intentions for human and creaturely existence. Repentance/faith involves no sacrifice of the intellect as is sometimes supposed; it is rather an awakening to understanding.

Act Three

The Exile

The land was given to us by our ancestors and we have every right over the land. This also applies to the river. I would like my children to know that the river is part of our life. What will happen to us when the clever men close the river?

Letter from a pastor in
Papua New Guinea

Chapter Eight

The Prophets

Prophets as Missionaries: Echoing the Call of God

We have noted before that with every repetition of God's promises for his people the scope becomes more comprehensive. Abraham was promised a land, a people and a blessing for the whole world. Moses mediates the promise for a particular kind of people that will enjoy a unique relation to the land (as specified in the law) and a new intimacy of relationship with God (as a "son," Ex. 4:22). Now David becomes king of a people inserted into the history of the nations, with a dominion over the land that issues in political and economic structures, and he is promised a house in which God will dwell. As the scope of the promised blessings increases, the breadth of responsibility of God's people increases proportionately. The kings had a greater responsibility to reflect God's law in the structures and institutions over which they ruled than did the judges. The lesson of the monarchy was that God wished to be honored in the political and economic spheres as well as in the social and religious. Whether we see it or not, there are spiritual battles being waged in these spheres as well. All of this must be borne in mind to fully comprehend the message of the prophets.

To gain perspective on the role of the prophet we must return to Deuteronomy 18, where the office of the prophet is initiated. Significantly it follows immediately the instructions given to the king in chapter 17 and to the priests (18:1-

8), and a warning of the paganism of the land into which they were going (vv. 9-14). In this context the prophet would be "raised up" by God to stand over against the priest and the king. "Prophet" here seems indefinite (it is without article in the LXX), and it seems clear that the ambiguity is intentional. It is made to stand both for the office of prophet that is being established, and for one prophet that will one day appear on the stage of history ("raised up" is best thought of in this sense). Interestingly the same Greek word is used of Jesus (Acts 3:26 and 13:33, which goes on to quote Ps. 2:7). Jesus was raised up onto the stage of history both as the king promised as David's son and as the prophet promised by Moses. God in Deuteronomy 18 goes on to specify that this prophet will speak "my words" (v. 18) in a way the people would heed. But whoever does not hear him, God himself would hold him responsible. That is, his word will take on the character of God's own voice which speaks and accomplishes what he speaks of. Truth will become known in the reality of a word that does not (cannot!) return to him void. This office of the prophet obviously began with Moses, but it also continued in the prophetic line. The NT pictures its fulfillment in the ministry of Christ and, as we will see, implies its extension in the missionary preaching of the Church (1 Cor. 2:13).

The classic confrontation between Elijah and Ahab in 1 Kings 21 makes clear that the prophet was made to stand before the king as the heir of the ancient covenant stipulations. Naboth did not want special treatment; he wanted to honor his land as his inheritance. The king by contrast wished to make it a commodity, something to be bought and sold. Jezebel urges him on with the classic characterization of kingship in the ancient Near East: "Do you now govern Israel"? (v. 7). In other words, can you not dispose of things as you wish? So while the kings confiscated the promises for their personal use, the prophets recalled them to their servant role. These were "men whose vision of God showed evil for what it was and displayed an energizing consciousness of a new order."[1] They called Israel to its ancient responsibility, to stand before God in the changed situation brought about by the monarchy. Again it was not the monarchy that was wrong, but what God's people had done with it. The prophets spoke against all that erected barriers against the individual's sense of being face to face with God.[2]

Prophets of the Eighth Century: Voices Crying in the Wilderness

1. *Amos*. Though a keeper of sycamore trees from Tekoa in Judah, Amos prophesied in the northern kingdom in the mid-eighth century B.C. Israel was in the greatest era of expansion since Solomon and felt secure. In a few years Tiglath-Pileser III would ascend the throne in Assyria (in 745) and begin his slow but inexorable march toward Israel and Judah. But for now there was peace, at least on the surface, though beneath the success and luxury of the upper classes there was oppression and a failure of justice.

> Woe to those at ease in Zion,
> and to those who feel secure on the
> mountain of Samaria. (6:1)

Is there anything special about you when compared to the nations around, Amos goes on to ask (vv. 2, 3). Woe to you who lie on ivory beds—you will be the first to go into exile (v. 7). For the first time Amos speaks the unthinkable, that God may judge his own people. Thus the first word of the prophetic "gospel" was one of judgment. It may be, as we will see, that God will not forget his people, but any mercy and blessing must come on the other side of judgment.

Why is this so? Because they trample the head of the poor into the dust and profane God's house with their indulgence (2:6-8); justice is perverted to serve the interest of the rich (5:7, 10-12); fraudulent commerce exploits the poor (8:4-6); there is unjust taxation (4:1). The key to this is that Israel is known by God (3:1, 2) of all the nations, and therefore they have a covenant obligation to acknowledge his

Lordship. This means that God intends his character to be reflected in the concrete life of the people: in their markets and courtrooms. But they had ignored their responsibilities even as they kept the rituals of the law. And because their wickedness had permeated into the structures of their society they stood under the judgment of God:

> Take away from me the noise of your songs;
> to the melody of your harps I will not
>   listen.
> But let justice roll down like waters,
>   and righteousness like an ever-flowing
>   stream. (5:23, 24)

Therefore God will punish them. Here Amos turns one of their cherished dogmas on its head. They believed that since God had fought for them in the past, he would intervene again if they were endangered. The day of the Lord was to them a precious assurance (something like "the return of Christ" to Christians today). Amos has to tell them:

> Woe to you who desire the day of
>   the Lord!
> Why would you have the day of the Lord?
> It is darkness, and not light. (5:18)

This is an astonishing idea! The day of the Lord recalled the holy war wherein God fought for his people. Is it possible that such a war can be fought *against* God's own people? Yes, it is. God will judge Israel (and Judah) along with the rest of the nations (as the oracles of chapters 1 and 2 show). Amos shows his roots in covenant traditions by noting that all the covenant curses will be brought against Israel (4:6-8), and in fulfillment of prophecy the land will vomit Israel out (7:17). How important is the land to Israel's life! Small wonder the king could not stand to hear this message and had Amos sent away (7:12, 13). Notice the reversal of verse 13. The Temple is of the kingdom; the king no longer serves the Temple!

The universal concern of God for the nations begins now to take clearer shape. The nations are liable to God's wrath not because they lie outside the sphere of his special revelation, but because he is their Creator and righteous judge. But there is hope. Amos gives us a first glimpse of the idea of remnant, a people rescued from God's wrath. If they seek God he will be gracious to the remnant (5:4, 14, 15). Then in the last chapter he speaks in barest outline of a rebuilding after judgment (9:13-15). The remnant is gathered for a special role: "that they may possess the remnant of Edom and all the nations who are called by my name" (v. 12). Here Amos recalls Balaam's promise (Num. 24:18) and introduces a "broader eschatological framework which transcended the historical perspective of the prophet,"[3] and which includes a distant hope for the nations.

2. *Hosea*. Also prophesying in the north in the mid-eighth century, Hosea exhibits a very close connection with the traditions of Deuteronomy. Thus the basic evil against which he spoke was the repudiation of Israel's covenant relationship. His context is the infiltration of Israel by the Canaanite fertility cults. In these ceremonies the cycles of vegetation were symbolized in mythical marriages with earth goddesses and attendant cult prostitution. According to B. S. Childs the central image is elaborated in the second chapter in which God himself is presented as the fertility God to "claim all the areas of fertility and kinship for Jahweh."[4] As it was assumed the gods affect the natural processes, Israel had to be reminded that her God transcended them all in his creative power. Israel has forgotten, says the Lord, "that it was I who gave her the grain, the wine, and the oil" (2:8).

As God suffered with Israel's unfaithfulness, Hosea is made to share God's grief by marrying an unfaithful woman. That is, Hosea is not only to speak the word of God, but to experience it in his own life—to become a "reproduction of divine disappointment" and thus open up the character of God in a new way.[5] The children of Gomer represent the judgment that will fall on Israel: *Jezreel*, for God will punish

Jehu for the blood of Jezreel; *Not pitied,* for God will have no more pity on the house of Israel; *Not my people,* for they were no longer God's people nor he their God (cf. chap. 1). Chapters 2 and 3 both give the full message of Hosea: they will return to the bondage of Egypt and experience a new exodus of salvation.

Hosea provides a new understanding of the treasure committed to Israel, which the NT will develop further. As eroticism stands at the center of Canaanite religion, so a new depth of love stands at the center of God's initiative to Israel (most movingly described in chapter 11). Since he is the God who delivered them, they are to "know" (acknowledge) no other God (13:4). Instead they forgot him and would perish for lack of knowledge (4:6). 4:1-4 lists the covenant conditions that have been broken, and 5:10 promises God's wrath will be poured out like water. Eichrodt summarizes: "We see how closely this destruction of Israel's political existence is connected with the betrayal of God to the nature powers, because both stem from the same root."[6] By the same token, the covenant which God will make will be with "the beasts . . . the birds . . . the creeping things" (2:18), but it will have the political effect that war will be abolished from the land and they will lie down in safety. All this will focus on a new moral relationship with God. Once again the promises of God include all of creation and the whole human community in its scope and will highlight the interrelated character of creation and re-creation.

3. *Isaiah.* During the same period in the south (c. 742-701), Isaiah prophesies in terms of the traditions associated with Jerusalem and the promise given to David (2 Sam. 7). Isaiah's encounter with God in the Temple is the interpretive key to his prophecies, for God's sovereignty and holiness come to clearest expression in Isaiah. There he saw God's final glory as already present throughout the earth (6:3). The whole earth *is* filled with God's glory, for he *already* reigns as King (v. 5). His vision makes him aware of his sin and he is cleansed, so that later he can see the light shining in the midst of the darkness all around him (9:2). The

Temple then is the focal point of the book and the place of God's glorious presence.

In the light of God's holiness, chapter 1 surveys the contents of the book. The situation is one of unrighteousness and thus of barrenness. Though the ox knows its owner, Israel does not know her obligations (1:3). Typically this lack of knowledge shows itself in oppression of the fatherless and widow (1:17) and in "grinding the face of the poor" (3:15). Because they have violated the covenant stipulations, their religious ceremonies have become an abomination to God. They must be purged and refined (1:18-24—notice how the imagery of the holy war is used of this judgment). The judgment that will fall upon Judah will be horrible:

> The Lord will smite with a scab
> the heads of the daughters of Zion. . . .
> My people go into exile
> for want of knowledge. (3:17; 5:13)

Yet Isaiah's confidence in the promises to David is so sure that he sees a rebuilding of the house of David which will accomplish all that God had promised David in 2 Samuel 7. At times the featured instrument of this rebuilding and re-gathering appears to be a righteous remnant; at other times it is a new David that will reign in righteousness; then again at times the two seem to merge, as later, with the suffering servant. The remnant is spoken of in the symbolic name that is given Isaiah's son, meaning "A remnant shall return" (7:3). This remnant will be called holy (4:3); they will not lean upon those who smote them, but upon the Lord (10:20); they will provide a refuge in Jerusalem (14:32); and though taking root in Jerusalem they will go out of Jerusalem (37:32). Here is barely hinted a mission in which God's righteous remnant will go forth from Jerusalem. But most interesting of all is the reference to a cornerstone or a sure foundation which God is laying in Zion, and which will be characterized by justice and righteousness (28:16, 17). Clearly this refers to the dynastic promises to David and recalls the "house" which God promised he would build for David with the seed that would sit on the throne. But it cannot be assumed that the reference is only to that ruler and not also to the righteous remnant. The ruler and the people stand in the closest relation.

The promises to David also lie behind that enigmatic prophecy in 7:14. Isaiah had just sought to dissuade Ahaz from making alliances with the nations around (a clear case of leaning on those who smite you!). To one convinced of God's sovereign direction, as is Isaiah, such a path would be foolish. The prophet goes on to promise a special sign: a special birth (a son!), recalling Genesis 3:15, the birth of Samson, and, of course, the promise to David. But this son will be Immanuel—that is, God with us. Though this must have had immediate reference to that time, the hope it raises is certainly better fulfilled in Christ the Savior.

No clearer picture of the political dimension of God's kingly rule is to be found than the great passage of Isaiah 9:6, 7: "Of the increase of his government and of peace there will be no end." As if to underline this dimension of God's rule, chapters 16 to 24 are given over to prophesying judgment upon the nations, a judgment punctuated with the refrain: "says the Lord of hosts." For God is the God of the nations— after Isaiah there can be no doubt of this. But now Jerusalem and the root of David (see 11:1-9) are more and more involved with the fate of these nations; what he opens none shall shut, and what he shuts, none shall open (22:21, 22). All of these themes focus on a new Jerusalem and a new ruler, whose rule will encompass not only the nations, but also the cow, the lion and the adder (11:8).

> For the earth shall be full of the
>   knowledge of the Lord,
>   as the waters cover the sea. (11:9)

And to this new Jerusalem all the nations will flow, for "out of Zion shall go forth the law, and the word of the Lord from Jerusalem" (2:3).

These prophets then emphasize that the failure of Israel and Judah is as complex in its effects as it is simple in its cause. They have no "knowledge"; that is, they have forgotten the loyalty that is due God in their special covenant relationship. They were still faithful in their worship, but they did not understand that worship outside of the righteousness which suited their covenant relationship was not pleasing to the Lord:

> He has showed you, O man, what is good;
> and what does the Lord require of you
> but to do justice and to love kindness,
> and to walk humbly with your God? (Mic. 6:8)

The characteristic sins became idolatry and oppression of the poor, and therefore God had to bring upon them all the covenant curses that Deuteronomy promises. For all these things are interrelated. They belong to the totality that God intends for his created order. Just as social injustice and barrenness of the land result from forgetting their covenant loyalty, so a renewed covenant would issue in a new possibility for social life and a new fruitfulness for the land. As Israel would soon have occasion to lament, the loss of the land was symbolic of the loss of everything; for land is not merely a setting of human life, it is one of the protagonists in the great struggle for righteousness. As the land was evicting Israel, so the new order God promises will be the fruit of the renewed earth (Isa. 4:2).

Chapter Nine

Eviction from the Land

A Scattering or a Sending?

By the seventh century Israel has gone into exile and Judah
is threatened. While the air is heavy with threatening disaster in the prophets of this period, there is no sense of accident or random misfortune. The coming calamities have a
specific cause. Their sins have made a separation between
them and God; so God is sending them out of the land. In
one sense their exile resembles the scattering of the people
after Babel. Jerusalem had become a proud boast for Israel
rather than the home of the humble and pure in heart. But
there is also a glimmer of a better sending that we will see in
Acts 8. For the sending of God's people into the nations is
ultimately for the blessing of all.

But we must not underemphasize the sense of ending
that the exile entails. The sense of doom is just as ominous as
the myths of chaos before creation or the oppression in
Egypt. There is nothing left to do but cry out, and Jeremiah
becomes a representative of God's people who cry out to
him in their suffering. For the prophets were willing to risk
the very existence of Israel rather than betray her spiritual
heritage.[1] So the best way to think of this act of God is to
consider it a preparation for a new creation, a new exodus,
which is the way Scripture presents it. For humanly speaking there could be no survival for Israel and Judah. Like
barren Sarah, or the slaves in Egypt, or the disoriented

wanderers in the wilderness, there seemed to be no future. Only the creative power of God gives any grounds for hope. Ultimately then this is simply a new time of wandering and a new opportunity to trust God.

In spite of this, we are entering the period that experienced the most glowing hopes of any period in Israel's history. As Hendrikus Berkhof has pointed out, the focus gradually changes in the OT from the past (the Exodus and entrance into Canaan), to the present (in the royal Psalms and the Temple worship), to the future in the prophets—the near future in the earlier prophets, the more distant in the later.[2] But throughout the past, events loom ever larger as types of what God will do in the future.

But now as Israel is scattered, the nations become more and more involved in her future. Their rulers become in fact God's anointed means of judging Israel (Isa. 10), though they also lie under God's wrath themselves (see Nahum). Throughout, it becomes gradually apparent that somehow in Israel's scattering and regathering lies the peace and salvation of the nations.

1. *Jeremiah*. Jeremiah begins his "ministry of articulated grief"[3] in 627 just as Asshurbanipal of Assyria dies and Judah regains her independence, and he continues to preach right up until the final destruction of Jerusalem in 587. King Josiah's reforms, begun soon after Jeremiah commences his ministry, may have encouraged the prophet for a time, but soon complacency and a creeping pagan influence are again evident. Then in 609 Josiah dies in battle and his son Jehoiakim reigns as an Egyptian vassal. Apparently he immediately followed Solomon's example and began to build himself a beautiful house, using forced labor. Jeremiah's response was a direct reflection on the law of the king in Deuteronomy 17: "Do you think you are a king because you compete in cedar?" (Jer. 22:15). Jehoiakim's father, by contrast, showed his kingship by doing justice and righteousness: "He judged the cause of the poor and needy; then it was well. Is not this to know me? says the Lord" (v. 16). You, Jeremiah goes on, have eyes only for dishonest gain! So God

will make this city a curse for all the nations of the earth (26:6). Small wonder that the priests laid hold of Jeremiah and said to him, You shall die, for you have spoken against Jerusalem! (26:8).

The book of Jeremiah reflects a direct clash of theologies. On the one hand there were the prophets who loved to remind the king that God had promised David's house would be eternal. Even though things might look bad for Judah, they could be sure that God would never allow it to be destroyed. Perhaps in 597 when the first deportation took place and Jerusalem was spared, they were quick to use this as proof of God's protection. In John Bright's discussion of these things he implies that these false prophets (see Jer. 23:16) may even have claimed to be disciples of Isaiah, though that prophet would certainly have repudiated their message of false comfort.[4]

Jeremiah, on the other hand, stands firmly in the tradition of Hosea and Deuteronomy: Israel's blessings are contingent upon their keeping the law (26:4, 5). In the famous Temple discourse (7:1-15) Jeremiah makes it plain that if they would truly amend their ways God would allow them to dwell in the land of their fathers. Meanwhile, the mere presence of the Temple would not save them (vv. 4-7). But now God will execute his fierce wrath and drive them from the land. Interestingly, the words of the oracle describing God's wrath recall the cosmic battle of the Exodus and of creation (see 4:13, 23-26), indicating that these events were to be another creative act of God—a creation that would be mediated through judgment.

This point bears emphasis. On the one hand the ending of 587 and the destruction of Jerusalem was complete. Jeremiah gave no grounds for being optimistic. When Zedekiah comes to the prophet and asks for some assurance that "the Lord will deal with us according to all his wonderful deeds" (21:2), Jeremiah has to answer that although God is in the war, he is on the side of the Babylonians! (vv. 3-6). The Davidic dynasty as they knew it was ending, and it would never be restored. "Being in the land without caring for community ends history."[5] But at the same time these awful events were themselves to become part of God's story with his people. As J. A. Sanders put it, they would be added as another chapter of the torah story.[6] This would lead to a new exodus. God still has plans of peace for his people, but these will only be realized through the suffering of exile. "For Jeremiah the exile is the fulfillment of the purpose of God: the exiles are blessed in their disaster."[7] But notice that they will be blessed only as they accept this judgment, settle down in their exile, and seek the peace of the city where God has sent them. Jeremiah says, "In its welfare you will find your welfare" (29:7). After this I will bring you back, says the Lord, and be found by you. For the promises to Israel and Judah are based on the order of creation itself and indeed are a reaffirmation of the intentions of that order (cf. 31:35-37, esp. v. 36). All this is portrayed in the image of the new covenant which the prophet gives us. But before we note this culminating promise of Jeremiah we must pause to examine the place of the prophet himself, the messenger, in all of this.

We have hinted that Jeremiah is fully involved in the grief of God; in fact, his complaints are recorded in embarrassing detail (chaps. 12 and 15). Why are these litanies of grief included? We have noticed from the time of the Exodus that the cries of God's people and God's response plays a central role in OT religion. These complaints, called laments, become a part of Israel's worship in the Psalms and come to their highest OT expression here and in Lamentations. As Sheldon Blank has pointed out, Jeremiah here becomes a paradigm of the man of God experiencing real personal anguish and longing, all of which comes to expression in his prayers.[8] But he is a type also in that he experiences real response from the Lord. The theology of Jeremiah, like all biblical theology, is dialogical. He even becomes, like Moses, an intercessor on behalf of his people (14:11; 18:20), and is made to share their judgment (16:8-13). Jeremiah's anguish with and for his people is surpassed only by the Suffering Servant of Isaiah (which some scholars believe was actually modeled after Jeremiah); both focus on the vocation of God's people. Israel's life is not only to be a bearer of its precious treasure, but an ensample of it, an experience that involves suffering. Blank concludes: "Israel's mission is so like that of a prophet that the servant's features are the features of a prophet: an ear to hear, a mouth to speak and a message to bring to the nations, prophetic torah to impart to the peoples of the earth."[9]

We are now in a position to understand Jeremiah's vision of the new covenant. Chapter 31 begins with the reference to "that time"—that is, after the new creative work which God will do, when he makes a new covenant (vv. 31-34). But note that the same God makes this covenant; the law is the same and the people are the same.[10] In what sense, then, is it new? It is new simply in that it will be kept. God will be working from both sides of the relationship: he will write the law on their hearts. That is, the people themselves will be renewed. The inward character of the new covenant and the personal communion with God that this implies is deepened and enriched by Jeremiah's own experience with God in the book. But notice that communion is to be the end of visible righteousness: "they will all know the Lord" (i.e., honor their covenant duties). For "to live in covenant requires obedience to the covenant stipulations."[11] It is this new covenant that is to be announced to the nations: "Hear the word of the Lord, O nations, and declare in the coastlands afar off. . . . For the Lord has ransomed Jacob" (31:10, 11); and it is the covenant that will be specially remembered and proclaimed in the Lord's Supper in the NT (cf. 1 Cor. 11:25).

2. *Ezekiel*. This prophet speaks to his people from the depths of the exile, having been taken to Babylon during the first captivity in 597. Like Isaiah, his prophecy rests on a towering vision of God (chap. 1). But this vision, whose imagery recalls Sinai and anticipates the symbols of Revelation, occurs "among the exiles by the river Chebar" (1:1), and not in the Temple. For the priest Ezekiel, the final horror was that the abominations of God's people had driven

God out of his sanctuary (8:6). God was himself in exile with his people! Like Jeremiah, Ezekiel suffers with and for his people (see the symbolic acts in 4:1—5:3); but he sees the glory of God in that suffering. He has been made a lookout for his people (3:17-21 and 33:7-9). Because of his vision of God he understands the worthlessness of the institutions of Israel and sees that God's commitment is not to these particular forms but to the purposes behind them. Now Israel has become an unfaithful wife (chap. 16) and has committed political adultery (chap. 23); her evil is radical. As Ezekiel's vision of God recalled Sinai, so does his vision of judgment (5:13 and 7:7). Both represent God coming forth in his revelation, and thus both show that "the ultimate meaning of God's action toward his people is to recognize God's revelation in this action."[12] And this too is the purpose of the judgment Ezekiel announces on seven nations (chaps. 25-32): their sin is determined by their attitudes toward God's sanctuary (25:3).

So God will act. The new mission on which Israel will be sent begins with this scattering. Note that it rests on the same ground as the original creation: the character of God. He will act "for the sake of my holy name" (36:22) which Israel has profaned among the nations. They have failed in their first mission; but God will send them on another. He will put his Spirit and a new heart in them (36:26, 27), an act which recalls Genesis 2:7 and his giving Adam the breath of life. This will focus on a new shepherd which God will give them. Who will this shepherd be? On the one hand God says he himself will be their shepherd (34:15), but on the other hand he also calls this leader his servant David (34:23). Here is the first glimpse that the king which will fulfill the promises of David will be God himself. This is further emphasized in the central imagery of Israel's hope, the valley of the dry bones in chapter 37. Nothing less than a resurrection—a new creation—is necessary to save Israel. But though this will be God's work, Ezekiel is asked to prophesy to the dead bones. The prophet then is actually a mediator and not only a herald of God's re-creative work. He speaks God's creative word. The book climaxes with a vision of a new Temple (chaps. 40-48), which becomes the setting for a new purified worship of God by his renewed and righteous people (cf. 37:22). The glory of the Lord reenters the Temple, and the land is again divided among the people. But this time: "You shall allot it as an inheritance for yourselves and for the aliens who reside among you. . . . They shall be to you as native-born sons of Israel" (47:22, 23). As God does his final redemptive work, the line between Israel and the nations breaks down.

New Symbols of Hope in the Midst of Crisis
From a human point of view this was the darkest point in Israel's history. For many it seemed that God had simply forgotten his promises to David: an eternal throne in a destroyed city? As John Bright says of this period: "Israel's very survival as a definable community was at stake."[13] Yet, as we have indicated, just at this time the prophets were able to offer new symbols of hope that grew out of (and expanded) their previous experiences. In his study of this period Walter Brueggemann observed with an insight relevant to every missionary: "Inversions may begin in a change in language, a redefined perceptual field or an altered consciousness."[14] What images can we discern through this darkness that promise the transformation we so earnestly hope for? Especially we wonder, where will the nations fit in?

First, it is clear that God is interested in the peace of the nations. In some deeply touching passages of Isaiah, it is implied that God hears their call just as he hears the call of his own people (Isa. 15:2-5). Moreover he is interested in their outcasts (like fluttering birds) and their scattered remnants (like scattered nestlings) and wishes that they find refuge (and justice) as they sojourn among Israel (Isa. 16:2-4). But now Israel herself is scattered among the nations. What is her role there? Again Jeremiah says, seek the peace of the city where you are, for their peace means your peace (29:7). God is clearly restless until his justice is displayed among the nations. So, as Richard Mouw points out, Paul's prayer for kings and those in authority (1 Tim. 2:1, 2) is prayed "in continuity with the OT vision of a righteous society."[15]

Second, it is also clear that God desires that the nations repent and be spared the judgment they deserve. There is no hesitation to speak against the wickedness around Israel (as Nahum speaks against Nineveh and Amos the nations), but Jonah gives us a bright picture of God's desire for those outside the covenant community. Though reluctant initially, Jonah goes and preaches to Nineveh; and the people repent. The story draws a very pointed contrast between God's heart and the preoccupation of his servant; Jonah is worried about a plant which he wants for its shade; God desires the salvation of the whole creation which he has made.

> You pity the plant, for which you did not labor, nor did you make it grow. . . . And should not I pity Nineveh, that great city, in which there are more than a hundred and twenty thousand persons who do not know their right hand from their left, and also much cattle? (Jonah 4:10, 11)

Finally it is evident that Jerusalem, when it is rebuilt, will become a praise among the nations. The prophets saw a great pilgrimage of the Gentiles to Jerusalem in the last days seeking rest and peace.[16] The most famous reference to this is Isaiah 2:2-4 when all the nations "flow to" Jerusalem. Micah, in speaking of building the walls, says the boundary shall be greatly extended, for "in that day they will come to you, from Assyria to Egypt" (7:11, 12). And Jeremiah predicts that "all nations shall gather to it, to the presence of the Lord in Jerusalem, and they shall no more stubbornly follow their own evil heart" (3:17).

But what instrument will God use to accomplish these purposes? How will Jerusalem be made a praise for all the earth? Of the means that the prophets speak of we chose two to describe: a servant and a son of man. The first focuses on the idea of the remnant, which has already appeared in our discussion of the prophets. Amos uses this in an ironic sense:

the remnant remaining to Israel will be a bit of an ear or a table leg! The remnant will be simply the "ruins" of God's people; what good are these? In a world falling apart, what can be the meaning of these few left after all the suffering? With insistence we are confronted with the picture of God's own people being made to suffer. D. N. Freedman reduces the theology of the exile to: "God loves Israel and Israel suffers."[17] The prophecy that addresses this question is that prophecy called Second Isaiah (Isa. 40—66), which may have been written by disciples of Isaiah during the exile. Of any portion in the OT, these chapters come closest to being a systematic theology.[18] As in the Exodus, all Israel is again poor (41:17-21); but these very people, these little ones, God has called as his servant, to be a light to the nations (41:9 and 42:6). But in order for Israel to fulfill this role they must be made to see that their God is the God of all creation, supreme among all gods (45:18-21). If he is one and over all, therefore the nations must find their rest in him (vv. 22-24). "Israel is God's witness solely by reason of its existence and of God's salvation which is given it."[19]

But note, there will be a new role for them to play in the further revelation of God which is now spoken of. In fact, this section begins with reference to a special coming of God (40:9, 10). A wholly new thing is taking place (43:18, 19): the Babylonian gods will be decisively defeated (46:1-4); the dry places will bloom, the creation will respond (41:17-19 and 51:2, 3); Jerusalem and the Temple will be rebuilt (44:26, 28); and many descendants will possess the nations (54:1-3, spoken of also as foreigners joining themselves to Israel; 56:3; 45:14—bringing their wealth!; 49:6 and 55:5). Notice that the familiar complex of events is associated with salvation: feeding the poor, destroying the false gods, creation blooming, and descendants enlarging their tents. In other words, the creative purposes will find their full expression because God is acknowledged and worshiped. For as G. E. Mendenhall notes of these chapters, political and economic concerns are present, but "they are the result not the cause of religious attachment to God."[20]

But our special focus is on the role of the servant of the Lord in this process. Is this Israel as a whole, or some individual or group within Israel? The truth is, we cannot say; the ambiguity is intrinsic to the passage. In fact, as Rowley points out, the servant is sometimes all Israel in its mission to the world, at times spiritual Israel and its mission to Israel and the world, and again sometimes an individual "whose work becomes the inspiration of the mission and the power wherein it can be achieved."[21] The section which focuses on the suffering of this servant is chapter 53. H. W. Wolff puts this quite properly in the context of the deliverance of a slave people from Egypt and the law of the king in Deuteronomy 17. The true ruler, in other words, is the one who turns the other cheek and takes the part of the weakest. Such a one will be victorious. Because "as a servant he does not seek his own justice, God made him Lord and will show him to be Lord."[22] Of course the Christian thinks at once of Christ, but as H. H. Rowley points out this is less a predicate of Christ than a classic expression of a reality that he fully enunciates.[23] This passage certainly played a central role in the ministry of Jesus and defined the work he came to do (Mark 10:45 and Phil. 2:5-11). But even while fulfilling this picture, Jesus did not do away with the ambiguity associated with the servant of the Lord; he rather extended it to cover the reality of the Church. For the Church itself is called upon to take the part of the weakest, to turn the other cheek and thus to triumph in Jesus' name.

Of course just as Christ is not left on the cross, so Isaiah does not end here. For chapters 60-66 speak of the end of history. As Freedman observes, to ask why the righteous suffer is also to ask how history works.[24] For the purpose of suffering is the redemption of the world, and the birth of the new heaven and new earth (65:17-25). But as Isaiah recognizes, this has to follow a decisive battle with the forces of evil (chaps. 63, 64). To understand this we turn to the second of God's instruments: the son of man of Daniel 7.

The visions of Daniel 7—12 represent a crucial anticipation of the visions given to John on Patmos. The vision of

God in 7:9, 10 has a clear parallel in Revelation 1. The remainder of the chapter contains a synoptic view of the nations' history and the consummation of that history. It tells us that "one day these powers will display the extreme of their blasphemous might."[25] These powers, of course, are prefigured in various historical nations, but rather than seeking to match these nations with the descriptions of Daniel (or of Revelation) it is better to understand them all in the light of God's program. In verses 13, 14 a person—a heavenly man—appears on the clouds and is given dominion. But again in verse 27 this same dominion is given to the "people of the saints of the Most High; their kingdom shall be an everlasting kingdom."

Now the dominion promised to Adam, and the rule promised to David and his seed, are joined in one who is called the Son of Man and in his people. We will see that Christ conceived of his mission in terms of Daniel's son of man, but Daniel already shows us that the events of history are not meaningless or random. History has now become "the terrain on which God executes his battle against the adversaries. The outcome of the battle is certain: It is anchored in creation. Every indication of God's superior power is also an indication of the coming kingdom."[26] The battle is the Lord's, but it becomes clearer with each act of God's great drama that his people are to be fully involved in the struggle. Nevertheless the great virtue of Daniel is to remind us that our work is ultimately God's. As B. S. Childs put it: "Daniel's radical stance calls into question all human endeavors of 'bringing in the kingdom' or of 'humanizing the structures of society.' Rather, this biblical witness challenges the faithful to be awake and ready for the unexpected intervention of God in wrapping up all of human history."[27]

It is important to recognize that both the image of the suffering servant and that of the son of man cannot be understood apart from their context in the exile. For it is the judgment of God's people and their scattering among the nations that makes possible the developing theology of suffering and of dominion. God was taking that disaster and shaping it into an image and vehicle of his merciful purposes.

Summary of Mission in the Old Testament

Perhaps we have come now to the place where we can summarize our discussion of mission in the OT. Clearly the primary actor in this drama has been God who has taken the initiative to reveal himself and show his glory, first through creation and then through the people whom he has called to be his own. He desires that his nature and purposes be revealed in the heavens (Ps. 19) and throughout the earth (Isa. 11:9). This is the beginning and end for which he calls his people to their particular vocation. The context of this calling is God's own creative and re-creative work.

Secondly we observe that the primary call coming to various individuals in the OT—from Abraham and Moses to Jeremiah and Ezekiel—is for the sake of the nation of Israel. The role of these individuals is primarily to announce God's will to his own people rather than to nations outside of Israel. The primary arena of the announcement of God's goodness in the OT was the congregation.

> . . . things that we have heard and known,
>   that our fathers have told us.
> We will not hide them from their children,
>   but tell to the coming generation
> the glorious deeds of the Lord, and his might
>   and the wonders which he has wrought.
>   (Ps. 78:3, 4)

To say that these individuals were called for the sake of the nation is to remind ourselves that God's primary concern is with his people as a whole. The covenant promises are for the nation, and it follows that the calling and gifts of individuals in that nation are for the sake of the whole of God's people (just as the gifts of the Spirit in the NT are for the edification of the body as a whole: Eph. 4:11-13).

By the time we come to the prophets it is clear that the

calling of Israel as a nation is for the sake of the whole world.
This, of course, is already implied in the promise to Abraham, but it is only made explicit in the prophets. The theological basis of this is most plainly seen in the towering
monotheism of Isaiah 45, but it is already implicit in the
shema of Deuteronomy 6:4. Israel then is to be preserved
(cf. Esther) so that she can mediate God's promises for his
creation as a whole. They are to exhibit a people, institutions
and a land which will reflect God's glory so that this can one
day be communicated to the whole earth and to all peoples.
Exactly how this will come about is only imperfectly seen in
the OT, but in the prophets it is evident that this will involve
nothing less than another creative work like the deliverance
from Egypt, though it will surely surpass that event in its
effects and scope.

Although Israel often did not understand this more inclusive role, it was clear from the beginning of her existence
that she must be open to the stranger and the foreigner. This
followed from the very nature of Israel's existence. They had
once been slaves in Egypt, and their father Abraham had
been a wandering Aramean (Deut. 26). As God had delivered Israel from bondage, it was most fitting that the stranger join himself or herself to Israel and thus proclaim the
greatness of her God. The Exodus included a mixed multitude of people—all who were anxious to escape the oppression of Pharaoh. Rahab the harlot was preserved and taken
into Israel (indeed she is given an honored place in James
2:25) for her hospitality to the spies. Many Canaanites were
included in David's court and welcomed into the course of
Israel's history. These, the prophets imply, are but firstfruits
of the day when many nations will take refuge in Jerusalem.

But these all look to Israel, not because she has some-
thing of her own to offer them, but because of what God has
done in Israel. From the beginning God's dealings with
Israel were of direct concern to the nations (Ps. 67:1, 2). As
Johannes Blauw puts it: "World history is a history around
Israel, just as Israel's history is a history around the works of
God."[28]

At the same time there is the awareness that the relation of Israel and her rulers to the nations will somehow involve their judgment. Mission, if it is to succeed, must involve conquest; there will be battles and casualties. For the struggle of God in history is with the powers of evil, and his people will become involved in this battle when they join themselves to him. Peace cannot come without a fight, healing without suffering.

This brings us finally to the pinnacle of the OT revelation of God's purposes: his own sharing in the sorrows of his people. From the beginning there is a confidence that God will hear the cries of his people when they are oppressed. This develops into the picture of God suffering for his people in Hosea and of his prophet suffering for his people in Jeremiah. Finally in the Servant Songs God's own servant (his people? his anointed?) will suffer a chastisement that makes for wholeness and healing (Isa. 53:6). There must be a suffering for creation before God's people and his creation can reflect God's renewed purposes for them.

But there is also a hint of a new cosmic ruling and dominion in Daniel 7. One like the son of man is given dominion so that all peoples, nations and languages should serve him (7:14). This dominion moreover is given also to the people belonging to this kingdom, so that all dominion and kingdoms shall serve and obey them (v. 27)! Those who join themselves to God then will share not only his suffering and his battle with the forces of evil, but also his rule over an everlasting kingdom!

The inward movement in the OT represents then a concentration of energies. It lays the foundation and sketches in the boundaries of a universal rule which is taken up and reinterpreted in the ministry of Christ. The OT prepares a universal message for what will become in the NT a universal mission.

Chapter Ten

Between the Testaments:
A Distant Hope

Does Salvation Lie in a Separated Community?
When the Persian king Cyrus put an end to the Neo-Babylonian empire and allowed the exiles to return in 539 B.C., the response was not overwhelming. The small dispirited band that returned to Palestine would not have mistaken the event for a new exodus. Even when a hundred years later a stronger initiative to consolidate the Jewish community in Jerusalem brought back Nehemiah, then Ezra, the emphasis was rather on preserving their traditions than advancing into the world.[1]

The continuing exile was the more important reality. The scattering of the Jewish people throughout the Near East (which came to be called the diaspora) was to be a permanent fact of Jewish consciousness: God's people were to be perpetually homeless, taking refuge among the nations. All the dangers and opportunities this provided must be the concern of this chapter. For some, the scattering seemed to threaten the very existence of the nation as a definable community. This inevitably gave rise to new attempts to become a separated people, the first under Ezra and Nehemiah. Much in this program was in continuity with the best OT traditions. Ezra, in introducing the public reading of the law (Neh. 8), called also for public confession (Ezra 9, 10). From henceforth this announcement and response was to constitute the central moment of Jewish life. Life was to center on the torah, which was given formal recognition under Persian law. To protect this new life of righteousness, Nehemiah and Ezra insisted on a strict enforcement of Sabbath laws (Neh. 13:15-21) and the statutes against intermarriage (Ezra 9:12 and Neh. 13:23-28). Perhaps Nehemiah 8—10 records the initial formation of what is called the Great Synagogue, which marked the origin of the traditions of the elders and the oral law which sought to adapt the ancient provisions to a changed situation. Prayers were regularized, festivals (such as Purim) were established, and the synagogue—the place for regular worship and study of the law—became a fixed institution of the diaspora. This whole program, however, was one of retrenchment; they sought to recapture the ancient confidence of long life in the prosperous land rather than reaching out for the high hopes of the later prophets.

Does Salvation Lie in Accommodation to the Surrounding Culture?

There were others, especially after the victories of Alexander the Great in the fourth century and the consequent influence of Greek culture, who felt the way ahead must be through adaptation to the culture around them. Perhaps they even recalled Jeremiah's advice to seek the peace of the nation where they were. In any case, most Jews never returned to the land and were forced to come to terms with their circumstances. Though scattered in small settlements throughout the Near East, they kept up their ties with Jerusalem and still looked upon it as the source of blessing and salvation and eventually began to pay the Temple tax regularly. At the same time, Hellenism began its subtle and widespread influence upon their thinking. They began to use Greek rather than Aramaic and in fact had the OT translated into Greek (the translation known as the Septuagint or LXX). Even the language of this translation reveals subtle shifts of understanding (scholars in fact have argued that it betrays a clear missionary intention). They also began to think through their traditions in the philosophical categories of Greek philosophy. In some places, notably Alexandria, this had a long-lasting effect on the character of Judaism.

While, as we will see, there were not lacking those who regretted this pagan influence, this openness provided the greatest opportunity for Jewish missions in the history of this people.[2] The Hellenism of this period displayed a deep religious longing that its own religious traditions were incapable of meeting. The people among whom the Jews lived were therefore hospitable to new ideas, and many heard readily the Jewish story and became God-fearers. Though this cannot be called a mission in the strict sense of the word, as there was little sense of being called by God to this work, it provided an important precedent for the Christian mission of the NT. These people represented a broad-minded accommodating stream in Judaism. While, as M. Hengel has pointed out,[3] there were strong pressures toward syncretism, and the urban and universal consciousness of Hellenism led to a laxness in keeping the law, this contact made possible the only attempt of Judaism to address the nations and served as an important means of influencing the whole of Western civilization with Jewish ideals.

Does Salvation Lie in a Transcendent Intervention of God Alone?

Many of course repudiated the very thought of such an accommodation. These still lived under the paralyzing shadow of exile and return. For some, this trauma had called into question the very idea that God is at work in history. As God's people who sought to keep the law, they thought of themselves as alienated from the world around and the object of derision and misunderstanding. It is among people like this that the movement which goes under the name Apocalyptic arose during this period. Daniel reflects thinking of this kind, and it can be found in books like Enoch and IV Ezra as well.

These people had come to believe in the radically evil character of this present age. They no longer could see how God's past acts, however wonderful, could lead to the future foretold in the later prophets. And when the disjunction between God's past acts and his future acts becomes too great, Paul Hanson notes, apocalyptic arises.[4] Though God's people must continue to keep the law, they cannot imagine that their efforts play any part in God's revelation of salvation. Thus the only hope lies in a new creative act of God in which this evil age is destroyed and a wholly new order is introduced. This led to the strict separation between conceptions of this age and those of the age to come that was to be so influential in later Judaism. The NT in fact has incorporated this idea of the two ages albeit in a surprising way. While these believers showed great confidence in God, they tended to abdicate all responsibility on the historical plane,[5] and there was no motivation to engage in mission of any kind. As G. E. Ladd puts it, Jewish apocalyptic thinkers forgot that the God who acts at the end of history also acts within it and reveals himself in and through historical events.[6] These ideas, however, had a large influence on the parties and sects we turn to next.

Does Hope Lie in Preserving a Purity among God's People?
1. *Essenes*. Throughout Jewish history there had been those who concentrated strictly upon keeping the law. This tradition, which came to be known as the Hasidim during the intertestamental times, came later to constitute the fundamental Jewish tradition. Some took this view to an extreme and concluded that purity entailed a strict separation from the surrounding community. During the Maccabean period (mid-second century) a teacher of such a group, called the Teacher of Righteousness, took the prediction of Isaiah 40:3 seriously and led his followers out into the wilderness to prepare for the Lord's coming. In settling along the shores of the Dead Sea in what is called today Qumran, they sought by study and discipline to create a perfect community of God's people who lead a sacred order of life and are completely conformed to the Mosaic covenant. Thinking themselves a fresh stem from the root of Judaism they wanted to lead a life of continuous worship that reflected the

heavenly choirs, maintaining ritual purity by daily washings. All of this was in order to make themselves pure for the final war of the children of light against the children of darkness, which they expected shortly and which would bring in the messianic age. Their mission was to keep themselves pure; they felt no responsibility for the world around them. Indeed, they were strictly forbidden from revealing to outsiders their books and way of life. While understanding much about God's holiness and the joy of true worship, they had lost the sense of God's universal desire for the nations.

2. *Pharisees*. More moderate heirs of the Hasidic tradition were the Pharisees, who became important by NT times. This was a scholarly class who thought of themselves as the true descendants of Ezra and who dedicated themselves to teaching the written and oral law—the latter developing through the attempt to extend the written laws to cases not covered by the law of Moses. They rejected the pessimism of the Apocalyptists and even supported for a time the Maccabean revolts, but gradually lost interest in such struggles. While they resented the Roman rule, they were willing to cooperate with it if they were left to teach and study freely. By the time of the NT they were legitimately sitting in the seat of Moses (Matt. 23:1-3) and zealously seeking to win converts to Judaism (Matt. 23:15). While their views about the Messiah were not clarified, they apparently sought to prepare themselves for the coming of the Son of David by purity and holiness of life. But their resulting views of ritual purity limited their contacts with outsiders.[7]

Their belief in the resurrection moreover led them to focus on the world to come as the place of salvation. However, their deep spirituality and commitment to the law made them the definitive influence on all subsequent Judaism and may even have influenced some of the formulation in the NT. E. Rivkin makes the interesting if exaggerated proposal that their threefold belief was taken over by Christianity. They believed that God so loved the individual that he revealed his twofold (written and oral) law to Israel, that whoever internalizes the law will inherit eternal life (cf. John 3:16).[8]

3. *Sadducees*. These belonged to the priestly and aristocratic class centering in the Temple. Though they supported the idea of a Jewish state, for obvious social and economic reasons they tended to support the status quo. In fact, they were more open to linking their views to those around them[9] and rejected the casuistry of the oral law (feeling, as priests, that they were capable of deciding on questions of interpretation).

4. These were all opposed by the *Zealots* who, though probably not forming a separate party, represented all those who insisted that only God could rule his people and all other rules must be resisted. Paying taxes was therefore a kind of idolatry for this group. In 6 A.D. Judas the Galilean led a revolt which fed on ancient holy war traditions. Though their methods were political, their goals were religious. "All their activities, military as well as political, had to do with the realization of God's rule."[10] As the rule of God would mean the destruction of his enemies, they thought it their responsibility to take initiative to defeat the enemies of God's rule.

Or Does Hope Lie in the Coming of a Messiah Who Will Deliver His People?

While the views concerning the Messiah were confused and diverse during this period, it can probably be safely said that there was no party that had no messianic hopes. For the focus of Jewish hopes when Christ appeared were less on the person of the Messiah—whoever he (or they!) might be—than on the restoration of the Jewish nation.[11] These hopes included a regathering of Israel to Jerusalem and a restoration of its institutions. Sometimes these hopes were in continuity with this order, sometimes they were transcendent. Always they included some notion of a battle with the forces of evil. The restoration is the important thing, and often the role of a messiah is quite vague. The call Israel felt in general was to accept the moral yoke of the kingdom by fulfilling the

commandments. By reciting the *shema*, says Rabbi Gama-
liel, "we accept the yoke of the kingdom."[12]

Of course there were legalistic elements, and there was
hypocrisy; the NT is clear about this. But recent study has
also underlined the spirituality of the Rabbinic traditions.
R. N. Longenecker concludes of the Rabbis at the time of
Paul: "The essential tension . . . was not primarily that of
legalism vs. love, or externalism vs. inwardness, but fundamentally that of promise and fulfillment."[13] That is to say,
this period is characterized by its waiting. Though their
hopes took different shapes and related in various ways to
this world order, they knew the law would be fulfilled and
Israel would be gathered. To this event they sought to witness by their life, and for it they waited with eager longing.

Act Four

Jesus Christ

The Mighty One, God the Lord, speaks and summons the earth from the rising of the sun to its setting.

Psalm 50:1

Chapter Eleven

Jesus Christ: The Coming of the Kingdom

As in Egypt, God's people waited 400 years and more, restless under the yoke of foreign rulers. The social problems and inequalities among God's people became even worse than those attacked by the prophets. "Great estates forced back the free peasant farmers, and the number of landless tenants increased, particularly after the time of Herod."[1] Israel longed for a new act of God's deliverance. God did not allow these hopes to go unfulfilled, though he answered them in surprising ways. He was about to bring all history into a single focus, all creation to a final aching for wholeness. He would fulfill their hopes in a way that opened new and wider horizons than Israel could have imagined. Part of this fulfillment would now lie in the commission Jesus would leave with his people and which would keep the whole earth and all its people in its field of vision. The surprises began when attention focused on a small village in Judea, where met—as the carol puts it—the hopes and fears of all the years.

Preaching the Kingdom: The Center of Jesus' Ministry
However this has been interpreted, there is no doubt among Bible students that the preaching of the kingdom of God stands at the center of Jesus' life and ministry. Again we do better to think of kingdom in the Eastern way as a dynamic rule rather than a spatial realm. In Jesus' teaching, it is the

sovereign rule of God in history that leads to redemption of the lost and restoration of the created order. It is an active ruling. "Only the God who proves himself master over all is true."[2] As Luther explained in his explanation of the first article of the Apostle's Creed, only that God is real who is able to create heaven and earth. In Jesus the God of creation, of the Exodus, of the judgment of exile is on the move again for salvation.

1. *The kingdom is future.* Jesus continued the teaching of the Jewish Apocalyptists that God would intervene to save the world at the end of the age. The rule of God is something that will come upon us completely apart from human mediation. The kingdom is not something visible to which one can confess allegiance, but it is the coming rule of God into which one may enter (Matt. 7:21-23). Making use of the apocalyptic imagery, Jesus implies that it will be a sudden appearing (Mark 13:26) that will catch people unprepared (Luke 17:26). At the same time, Jesus taught that it would come within the lifetime of his hearers: "There are some standing here who will not taste death before they see that the kingdom of God has come with power" (Mark 9:1). So the great event for which the nation of Israel earnestly longed was coming near. In fact, at the beginning of his ministry Jesus went so far as to say that the kingdom was "at hand" or "has approached" (Mark 1:15 and Matt. 3:2).

2. *The kingdom is being manifested in the present.* As the ministry of Jesus proceeded, it became clearer what Jesus meant by this enigmatic announcement. On the occasion of a visit to Nazareth (Luke places it at the very beginning of his ministry) Jesus read from the prophet Isaiah in the synagogue. Quoting from Isaiah 61:1, 2 he announces:

> The Spirit of the Lord is upon me,
> because he has anointed me to preach
>   good news to the poor.
> He has sent me to proclaim release to
>   the captives
> and recovering of sight to the blind,

> to set at liberty those who are oppressed,
> to proclaim the acceptable year of the
>   Lord. (Luke 4:18, 19)

When he had finished he said simply: Today this is fulfilled in your hearing. There is a great deal of significance to this event, but two comments above all should be made. First, Jesus picks up the imagery of the jubilee year from Isaiah.[3] The prophet had looked forward to a final jubilee in which the suffering of God's people and the barrenness of the land would be healed. In speaking as he did then Jesus was saying that the final period of time in which the cosmic breach introduced by sin would be decisively healed *was now dawning*. It was no longer somewhere in the future, but it was present in his own ministry.

But second, Jesus announces the acceptable year of God's mercy, while leaving out the second half of the verse which goes on to say, "and the day of vengeance of our God" (Isa. 61:2b). In other words, the age that is now dawning is one in which the poor and suffering will find mercy with the Lord rather than experiencing his wrath. The judgment which is postponed has made way for a special period of hope. Here Jesus detaches the nationalistic idea of revenge due the nations from the hope of redemption, and promises the one without the other.[4] No wonder the Jewish audience was enraged! Here Jesus introduces a wholly new message of hope that lies in the announcement itself ("fulfilled in your *hearing*") and which will characterize the message of those Christ entrusts with his mission to the nations.

Christ also points out that the power of the kingdom is present in his mighty works, especially those which do battle with the forces of evil. When the Pharisees accuse Jesus of being in league with Satan, he answers sharply: "If it is by the Spirit of God that I cast out demons, then the kingdom of God has come upon you" (Matt. 12:28 and Luke 11:20). Of this passage in Luke, I. H. Marshall comments: "The kingly and saving power of God has drawn near to the hearers and is there for them to grasp."[5] The Jews looked forward to the binding of Satan at the end of the age, but Jesus insisted that this was actually taking place in the present in his own ministry (Matt. 12:29). This aspect of Jesus' ministry is widely recognized by NT scholars. W. G. Kummel notes: "Jesus characterizes his preaching as good news of the end-time . . . his deeds and words as the salvation event of the end-time."[6] Zero-hour has now arrived, affirms C. H. Dodd. In Jesus we see "God himself exercising his royal power."[7]

3. *The kingdom is present, but it is also coming.* Some of the most graphic teaching of Jesus concerning the kingdom is to be found in the parables (see especially Matt. 13). There the kingdom is presented under a double aspect, both as present and as future, especially in the parables of the mustard seed and the leaven. Both stories refer to the fact that the beginning of the kingdom may seem insignificant— none of the Jewish leaders received Jesus officially, and even his family and disciples did not really understand what he was doing. But in spite of this the kingdom will one day have a world-embracing significance. Professor Jeremias comments of these parables: "Out of the most insignificant beginnings, invisible to human eye, God creates his mighty kingdom, which embraces all the peoples of the world."[8] The small seed will grow into the largest of the shrubs in which the birds of the air—all the nations—will come to take refuge (Mark 4:30-32; recall the image of Isa. 16:2-4). Jeremias has rightly argued that the process or means of growth is not in view; we should not think of some kind of inevitable development or evolution. However, as Hermon Ridderbos points out, one cannot leave out of account the continuous effect of the kingdom. The word of the gospel has a totalitarian character that will have cosmic consequences.[9] This image of miraculous increase gives us a view of "eschatology in process of realization"[10] in the person of Jesus.

Perhaps the best way of understanding this double aspect of the kingdom is the picture given by Geerhardus Vos.[11]

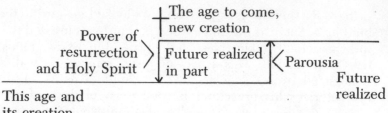

This age and
its creation

That is, though the kingdom will be fully manifested in the
age to come when Satan and his angels will be destroyed
(Matt. 25:41), this present age has already become the scene
of the decisive battle between the powers of evil and that of
the kingdom (Gen. 3:15 and Col. 2:15). Since this battle has
been won by the overwhelming power of Christ and displayed in the cross and resurrection, and since this power
has been poured out on the Church through the gifts of the
Holy Spirit, the firstfruits, the initial blessings of the kingdom can be enjoyed now. Thus we live in two ages at the
same time.[12] Most importantly, as we will see, it is mission,
the active proclamation of the kingdom reality in the gospel,
that fills up this overlap and gives it its meaning.

Manifestation of the Kingdom in Christ's Work: Preaching Good News to the Poor

Now we need to inquire into the character of this kingdom.
If our message is the gospel of the kingdom, it is essential
that we understand the nature of the rule that Christ has
introduced. In a word we can say: Jesus has come to extend
God's call to the poor, the lost (Mark 2:17). Repeatedly Jesus
insisted that he came to save sinners, those who were lost or
helpless. Now we are used to hearing that this refers primarily to those whose moral qualities exclude them from the
kingdom. Jeremias describes them as "those whose religious
ignorance and moral behavior stood in the way of their access to salvation according to the convictions of the time."[13]
This moral reference cannot be excluded, but it is hard to
avoid the conclusion that additionally Jesus was referring to

those whose social or physical condition forbade them from entrance into the religious establishment. Let us note some of the evidence for such a view. When John sent his disciples to ask whether Jesus was the one who was to come, Jesus replied (again quoting from Isaiah's visions of the end-time in 29:18, 19):

> Go and tell John what you hear and see: The blind receive their sight and the lame walk, lepers are cleansed and the deaf hear, and the dead are raised up, and the poor have good news preached to them. (Matt. 11:4, 5)

The last phrase may be taken as a summary statement of the whole: those who are in a situation of helplessness are being promised deliverance. The beatitudes, which come close to being a synopsis of Jesus' entire teaching, begin (in Luke which accurately portrays the meaning even if it is not original): "Blessed are you poor, for yours is the kingdom of God" (6:20). After a lengthy study of these and other passages, Hermon Ridderbos concludes that what is intended by poverty here is both a religious-ethical situation and a social position. [14] In perfect continuity with the OT tradition, these are those who cry out to God from a situation of helplessness. The significance of the gospel Jesus preaches is that as God heard the cries of his people in Egypt, as he heard the cries of the Psalmist and of Jeremiah, he is again hearing the cry of those who are hungering and thirsting for deliverance, those who look forward to "God's redemption of his people from the power of oppression and injustice that is continued for the present." [15] It is precisely this life-hungering for justice that characterizes those who heard Jesus gladly.

In preaching to the poor, moreover, Jesus is showing most clearly his kingly power. Just as God's king is to side with the poor and needy and protect the helpless and so show his true greatness (see Ps. 72), so in his servant character Jesus reveals his true greatness, a greatness that features a cross as his coronation (see Phil. 2:5-11). Sadly, the Jews of his time failed to see how biblical was Jesus' ministry. For, as J. Sanders expressed it, if God huddled with the slaves in Egypt can he not also slouch in a cradle in Bethlehem?[16] Having spoken of its general characteristic, let us see if we can articulate this quality further.

1. The kingdom Jesus preached involved a new personal intervention of God himself that was to lead to a new intimacy of relationship with his people. The ancient promise that he would be their God and they his people was to find a new and richer fulfillment. This relationship, Professor Jeremias believes, centers on the single word "Abba," which appears often on the lips of Jesus.[17] Although it was God's desire to be a father to his people, we have no example in the OT of God being addressed as Father, and certainly not as "Abba" (which was the family word for "Dad" used as an expression of courtesy in Jewish homes). Yet this word which Jesus always used in his prayers expresses the heart of Jesus' relationship with God. Moreover, it lies at the heart of Jesus' own mission to communicate this intimacy of relationship to his followers as well. Because no one knew the Father as he did, he alone could communicate this relationship (Matt. 11:27), and so he was uniquely suited to call the weary and heavy-laden to find rest in him as though they were coming to God himself (as indeed they were!—see 11:28). Here is a relationship that transcends even that known by Adam and Eve in the garden and which the rest of the NT dares to call "sonship" (Rom. 8:14-17 and 1 John 3:2).

2. The kingdom Jesus brought, as in the OT, focuses on specific events in which God is acting for the salvation of the world. Mark, which focuses more on the work than the teaching of Jesus, records an interesting exchange in which early in his ministry bystanders accuse Jesus of giving a new teaching (1:27), saying: "With authority he commands even the unclean spirits, and they obey him." Here indeed is a new event! One which God is adding as another chapter in the great narrative of his creative and re-creative work.[18] These miracles and the final miracle of the cross are events in which Christ is delivering the weak as he binds the strong

man and plunders his house (note the two sides of judgment: punishment and restoration). So now in Jesus the powers of evil have found their grip loosened and the mighty work of restoration has begun. While the Rabbis looked forward to God's future deliverance, Christ was bringing about a radical change of tense and the powers of the future were being manifested in the present. These powers, however, appear in the most unlikely person of a Galilean carpenter who, we have noted, sided with the weak and oppressed. This servant character gave to the final event (that for which Christ entered history) its unique character. For it was through the cross, where God's holiness is preserved and the powers of evil defeated, that Christ achieved his special glory. So the central event, which is the new exodus, is the place where sin is dealt with and evil overcome. We return to this central theme below in our study of Mark.

3. The kingdom also marks the emergence of a renewed creation. After centuries of failure and discouragement, God's people finally witnessed the arrival of a new order of reality, mediated through one person: the Last Adam. After years of waiting, something was again *happening* in Israel. Striding across the landscape came one who with a word or a flick of a hand began changing things. His miracles then ought not to be seen as illustrations of his teaching but as part of the proclamation itself. Jesus' miracles rendered "visible the restoration of creation, and so the all-embracing and redemptive significance of the Kingdom."[19]

Note, however, that Jesus' teaching and miracles were in the first place not a denial of the created order, but a reaffirmation of it. As C. H. Dodd points out, Jesus' teaching, from his parables to the sermon on the mount, features the integrity of creation. As in the wisdom literature, to which Jesus' teaching is related, the principles of behavior "fall within a universal order established by the creation."[20]

At the same time Jesus reveals a new creative power which began to redeem creation, doing battle with the forces that threatened to destroy it, and in the process introducing a new order which will eventually displace the old. With a command, angry waves are stilled, fishes fill the net and spirits flee before him. As the parable of the unshrunken cloth shows (Mark 2:21, 22), this new order has broken in and will break apart the old. The kingdom then represents a new creation which perfects and extends the old and maintains its essential nature, even as it makes possible new dimensions of fellowship with God and humanity.

4. As the kingdom is a perfecter and not a destroyer of creation, so mankind in the new order is meant to experience the full provision of human need in all its dimensions. It is characteristic of Jesus' ministry that he met his hearers at the level of their need. He used their point of need as a means of establishing relationship and eliciting faith. Where there was hunger, he fed them; where there was suffering, he healed; where openness, he taught them. Miracles like the feeding of the 5,000 should be seen in analogy with the Exodus as an enacted parable signifying God's intention for creation. Hunger, disease and demonic oppression are all a violation of God's promise for creation and are all dealt with in the ministry of Christ.

This can be further seen by Christ's teaching to trust in God and not our abilities alone to provide for ourselves materially. The entire context of Matthew 6:33 implies that it is God's will that our need of food and clothes be met—indeed they may be supplied with the splendor of the lily and the dignity of the bird. But supplying these things is not to become our primary concern. Christ goes on to teach his disciples to pray for their daily bread in the same breath as it were as their prayer for the kingdom itself (indeed the implication is that the two are related). The prominence Jesus gives to the banquet as the picture of salvation, and his notoriety as a glutton, indicate that this dimension of human life was to him an important sign of God's presence. (Jeremias points out that the idea of eating and drinking mediating the vision of God is important in Scripture.[21])

Socially and politically it is clear that a new human potential is introduced by Christ's appearance. From both the OT and the teaching of Christ we learn that "the fulfillment of God's covenant would affect the social and historical life of men, of persons-in-community."[22] This follows from the fact that our acceptance with God is related to our accepting our brother, our forgiveness by God tied to our forgiving our brother (Matt. 5:24, 25). It follows that when God makes possible a new depth of relationship with himself, and a new permanency of fellowship, new dimensions are opened as well for human community. Moreover, our meeting of the needs of our brothers (Matt. 25:31-46) and our hospitality toward those in need (Jas. 2:18-26) becomes in the NT a sign of our membership in this new community.

Politically it is true that Christ did not directly challenge the Roman Empire, but as Karl Barth insists, because of Christ's authoritative claims (Matt. 28:18) it is not possible for us to conceive of any "political realm that would not be included in the Kingdom of Christ."[23] As in the case of OT institutions, the gospel does not attack the political structures directly but introduces a new reality that must eventually transform these structures. In the Gospels Jesus sets the limits in which the kingdoms of this world will function (Luke 20:25), thus challenging the universal claim of the Roman (or any other) government. He does not hesitate to point out the moral failings of its rulers and consistently sides with the victims of its oppression.[24] Finally the inviolable seal of the Emperor himself is broken as Christ emerges from the tomb and sets about to establish his universal reign. As we will see later, it is impossible to miss the political fallout of Mark 13:3-34 and of Revelation.

All of this comes within the scope of Christ's work, which deals with the problems of sin and death in the comprehensive context of a new creation. It is often pointed out that the OT features the physical and material aspects of salvation while the NT deals with the problems of death and alienation. But it is difficult to see how the latter problems can be dealt with apart from the former. We have noticed often the interrelated character of reality and the holistic nature of God's purposes. NT believers have no less need of eating and drinking than those in the OT! The key of course is to remember that the central image of renewal in the NT is the resurrection of Christ. There the righteousness of God is vindicated while the creation is renewed. Surely Christ's death and resurrection deal with the central problem of sin and alienation, but in dealing with that God has made possible a whole new level of peace in the created order as well.

The Kingdom Calls for a Personal Response

The advent of Christ's kingdom is something before which one cannot possibly remain indifferent. It is true that the kingdom is God's work. We do not bring it upon ourselves by keeping the law (did the people of Israel create the Exodus by obeying the law?). But this reality is something that can be missed; one must make a proper response to it (remember that where there was no faith, Jesus could do no mighty work).

The response must always focus on the person of Jesus. In his day (and ours!) entering the kingdom had to do with the stance that one took toward him (see Matt. 11:6). Faith had to be placed in him in order to experience the power of the kingdom. Jesus speaks of entering the kingdom like a little child (Mark 10:15)—that is, "simply and naturally without making any claims."[25] C. H. Dodd adds, "It is learning to think of God as your father and of yourself as his child quite simply."[26] But this is also pictured as a decisive commitment that allows nothing to hinder, a selling everything, without turning back (Matt. 5:30; Luke 9:62; and Matt. 10:37). This is summed up in the idea of repentance, stressed both in John's preaching (Luke 3:10-14) and in Jesus' (Matt. 4:17). To repent is to turn around, to change one's mind and one's life (both are included in the NT use of the word).[27] The proper response to the kingdom then involves a reorientation of one's values in accordance with those of the kingdom. When Zacchaeus promised to restore what he had defrauded, Jesus observed, "Today salvation has come to this house" (Luke 19:9).

While nothing we can do will bring the kingdom, our response must correspond to its reality. This is underlined in the sermon on the mount (Matt. 5—7), which encourages us to reproduce the "quality of God's action toward his children, and to pursue the direction in which that action points."[28] The results will be a community in which the hungry are satisfied (Luke 6:21) and enemies are loved (Matt. 5:43-48) and which is free of worldly cares (Matt. 6:25-34). All of this of course reflects the character of Jesus himself, but it also represents the fulfillment of the intention of the OT law (see Matt. 5:17).

This claim which Jesus makes on us discourages us from seeking to follow him in some more limited way. John Howard Yoder, for example, believes that we are called to reflect Jesus only "in his cross"—that is, in his revolutionary subordination to the powers.[29] As Richard Mouw has argued,[30] this ignores the links that the cross has with the OT promises and with events yet to come, all of which give the cross its meaning. The cross in this context represents the decisive victory over the powers of sin and death, and this fact (and the resurrection which followed!) makes it unnecessary for us to go the way of the cross (though we must still go the way of servanthood). The redemption and restoration Christ came to bring about and the gifts he gives the Church leave their imprint on the world as a bomb leaves its crater. It is this reality and its character that we are called on to respond to and reflect. We shall have more to say along this line later.

All this follows from God's intention to work from both sides of the relationship (as Jeremiah and Ezekiel saw). The announcing of the gospel itself has a unique efficacy which brings results. The parable of the patient husbandman (Mark 4:26-29) indicates that the harvest and the fruit will come when the time is ripe for them. The word sent out is the authoritative word of Christ, and so it will bring about results. "The preaching of the gospel is itself the guarantee of

the ultimate coming of the kingdom. It brings the latter
irresistibly nearer."[31] In this preaching God is calling out a
new people who will reflect him by responding to him in the
context of creation. The covenant task to which they are now
called is to proclaim and show the kingdom in their individual and corporate lives. But the basis of this calling lies in
the fact that the divine prophet has himself fulfilled the
covenant purposes of God. For he responded to God in the
context of creation with an obedience that perfectly reflects
God's character and completely fulfills his promises.

But all of this is still in the future, and we are getting
ahead of our story to speak of it now. Jesus, in fact, consistently told his disciples to tell no one what they had seen
until he had been raised (Mark 9:9); meanwhile they are only
to echo his call for repentance. This reticence is to be understood as follows: until those events take place, there is really
no gospel to preach. The powers of the kingdom are present,
but its full reality has not yet appeared. To emphasize this
point we turn to the book of Mark.

Chapter Twelve

The Death and Resurrection of Christ

In addition to giving attention to passages dealing with mission, we need to remember that the Gospels as a whole were written with a missionary purpose. This is more obvious in the case of Luke and John (Luke 1:1-4; John 20:31), but it is just as true for Matthew and Mark. These were written not only to strengthen the faith of early believers but to assist in their presentation of Jesus to outsiders. Moreover, the specific missionary commission given to the disciples in each Gospel must be read in the light of the particular purposes of that evangelist. The missions thrust of Mark, Matthew and Luke we examine in this chapter, leaving John, which was written later, to the chapter on the early Church.

Mark: The Death of Christ as an Enacted Rite of Salvation
The Gospel of Mark has been called a "narrative parable of the meaning of the life and death of Jesus."[1] The whole book is carefully constructed to show that the passion and death of Christ is the primary perspective that gives meaning to all other traditions about Jesus.[2] Jesus is presented as the Son of God (1:1) who is made to suffer and die in order to bring about redemption, and whose followers must be prepared to follow his path of humble service in order to reach true greatness (10:35-45). This blunt straightforward message may have been the Evangelist's way of attracting the attention of the indulgent Roman world.

1. *1:1-13, The prologue*. Mark begins his Gospel with the ministry of John the Baptist to show that "Jesus belonged to Jewish expectations of God's rule, and indeed that he was the fulfiller of them."[3] Following baptism by John there is the heavenly announcement of Jesus' vocation as Son and the demonstration of that call by his temptation in the wilderness. Jesus' "expulsion" into the wilderness recalls Adam and Eve's expulsion from the Garden (the same Greek word is used in Gen. 3:24, LXX) and Israel's sojourn in the wilderness and prepares for the regainment in the gospel. "Paradise is restored, the time of salvation is dawning."[4] So the stage is set for Jesus' ministry in Galilee.

2. *1:14—8:26*. Following Hahn's outline[5] we consider first Jesus' work among the people. Immediately following the programmatic statement of Jesus' message (1:14, 15) to which we have referred previously, the Lord calls his disciples to become fishers of men (v. 17). Interestingly the image of fishers comes from Jeremiah 16:16, where they seek out those due judgment. Here his followers are put at once "into Jesus' own service of proclamation and mighty acts."[6]

Jesus sets about at once to show the reality of the kingdom through his miracles (which are given more prominence in Mark than his teaching). In spite of these wonders, or perhaps because of them, there is a progressive rejection of Jesus not only by official Judaism, but also by his own family and even his disciples. Though his mission is first among his own people (7:27), crowds come to him from all over (3:7, 8), even the Gentile territories; and following rejection by the Jews he turns to the Gentiles (5:1-20 and 7:24). In Mark, the world pilgrimage of peoples focuses not on Jerusalem but on Jesus himself.

3. *8:27—10:45*. In this section Jesus concentrates on preparing his disciples for their ministry. Beginning with Peter's confession (in Gentile territory!) he explains the necessity for his death (8:31). But the disciples will not accept such a thought. Even the heavenly announcement at the transfiguration does not enlighten them, and they are urged to keep silence until the resurrection (9:9). On the beginning

of his trip to Jerusalem (10:32) he repeats his prediction of his death, and his disciples argue about who will be greatest. Jesus will later (in 14:62) identify his work with the Son of Man, but now he proceeds to explain this in terms of a particular vocation of suffering and death. That is, though he inaugurates the kingdom with his mighty power, his authority will be uniquely displayed in his ministry of suffering as a ransom for many (10:45, which recalls the suffering servant of Isaiah 53). Christ will exercise his dominion, but this will be particularly manifest in his role as the suffering servant (cf. Phil. 2:5-11). Moreover, this chapter makes it clear that the same things should be true of those who follow him: "Whoever would be great among you must be your servant" (10:43). For "the story of Jesus is also to be the story of his followers."[7]

4. *10:46—16:8*. The final rejection and crucifixion of Christ reveal at the same time the universality of the kingdom thus established. Jesus now continues his pilgrimage first to Jerusalem (this motif must have been a common one in Gospel traditions), and then to the Temple where he proclaims: "My house shall be called a house of prayer for all the nations" (11:17, quoting Isa. 56:7). Then during the trial when he stands alone before Pilate he boldly applies the prophecy of Daniel 7:13 to himself (14:62)—and those who hear spit on him and strike him (v. 65)! It is while hanging on the cross that the reality of his mission as son is acknowledged—by a centurion (15:39). But the disciples still are afraid when the Gospel ends in 16:8 (at least according to the oldest manuscripts).

Clearly it is the death of Christ that is Mark's focus, and it would be well for us to reflect on the significance of this. To do so, we must return to the famous Olivet discourse in Mark 13. Here, using apocalyptic imagery familiar to his hearers, Jesus lifts the curtain on events at the end of the age. For our purposes we need only note that the coming day of the Lord's judgment will involve wars, sacrilege, frightful portents in the natural order and the persecution of God's people. The whole created order and all political and social structures will be involved in this great final struggle. Second, while many of the signs were meant to refer to the end of the age, it cannot be doubted that some would take place soon (and a sampling of them within their generation, v. 30). Verses 24-27 speak of Christ's coming again, with accompanying signs which recall the darkness of the cross and the ascension on the clouds of his first coming. That is, Jesus implies that these final events of history were beginning in his own ministry, especially in his death and resurrection. Finally we notice that the role of the disciples amidst their persecution is the witness they bear, for "the gospel must first be preached to all nations" (13:10) before the end comes. And verse 27 speaks of the divine side of this mission as God sends his angels to gather his elect from the ends of the earth. This gathering, which begins in the mission of the church, is the historical manifestation of Christ's exaltation in power and is one of the signs of the last days.

The first significance of Christ's death then is that it initiates the last days by engaging the forces of evil in decisive battle, a struggle in which by the darkness and earthquake creation itself is shown to be involved (15:33 and parallels). Then immediately before the confession of the centurion, Mark emphasizes that the Temple curtain is torn (15:38), indicating that a new intimacy of access to God is now offered to all. While this becomes clear only in Paul, Mark further emphasizes that Jesus' death is delivering many from bondage to sin and death and bringing them into full fellowship with God (the allusion to Isaiah 53:11, 12 is inescapable in these verses and in 10:45). Here then is Christ, the Last Adam, bearing as man (God's creation, the seed promised the woman), "the full impact of his Father's holy wrath,"[8] and so sealing the new covenant with his blood.

While the great commission in Mark is probably not original (and may represent a second-century catechetical summary), it represents very ancient traditions and must certainly be taken into account. It continues the theme of the disciples' lack of faith (16:13) for which Jesus scolds them (v. 14). They are now instructed to go into all the world and preach to every creature (perhaps the whole creation or to all people in creation). Then the judgment inherent in preaching the gospel is explained: those who do not believe will be condemned. That is to say, Jesus' death marks the judgment upon sin for those who accept the good news, while those who reject him must bear their own judgment. Then Christ promises that signs will accompany the preaching of the gospel. The restored dominion won by Christ will be reflected in his people, especially in their proclamation of the gospel. And a special promise for their safety is included—interesting in a gospel which has promised persecution for Christ's messengers (13:9, 13). The account concludes by saying that after the Lord Jesus was taken up into heaven (cf. 13:26), "the Lord worked with them and confirmed the message by the signs that attended it" (14:20).

Mark then portrays the death throes of the defeated powers of darkness and extends the shadow of that struggle to the end of the age. In the striking image of Oscar Cullman,[9] the remnant of Israel has been narrowed now to one Person, who is rejected by all his followers and hangs alone on the cross. Yet this darkest hour is not the defeat but the victory of God's program; it is the absolute midpoint and fulcrum of redemptive history. This point will hereafter define the character of creation and history, and the response of people to this event will be determinative not only for their lives and destinies, but that of their families, communities and even of creation itself. Now this remnant will grow, first to include Christ's disciples and then, through them, representatives of every nation under heaven.

Matthew: Jesus, God's Messiah, Is the New Israel
An examination of the structure of Matthew reveals that it is based on an historical movement that culminates in the commission of 28:18-20. The threefold division we follow is based on the work of J. D. Kingsbury.[10] Matthew, writing for a Jewish audience, emphasizes that Jesus is God's promised Messiah through whose words and deeds God reveals the new order of his salvation.

1. *1:1—4:16*. The first section introduces the person of

the Messiah and his OT heritage. This continuity is stressed in verse 1, where Jesus is called the son of David and the son of Abraham, and in the genealogy which follows. This sonship is further defined in the birth narrative as the divinely conceived one who will save his people from their sins (v. 21) and will be "God with us" (v. 23). In chapter 2 Jesus is shown to be the king of the Jews to whom the foreign wise men (perhaps from Persia) come to pay tribute and give gifts. As in Mark, the pilgrimage of the nations focuses not on Jerusalem but on Jesus himself as the one destined to sit on the throne of his father David.

This aspect of Matthew's narrative underlines Jesus' significance not only as the fulfiller of OT promises but even more importantly as the personification of the nation of Israel. This is evidenced by Matthew's treatment in the remainder of this section. Jesus repeats Israel's experience by going down to Egypt (2:15), by fulfilling all righteousness stipulated by the OT (3:15) and finally by proving his faithfulness in the wilderness (chap. 4). The section concludes with Jesus coming to Galilee, where he will begin his public ministry and where the people who sit in darkness (even the Gentiles!) are seeing a great light (4:15, 16).

2. *4:17—16:20*. In this portion Jesus proclaims the kingdom of heaven to the Jews (since Matthew is speaking to a Jewish audience, he substitutes the term kingdom of heaven for the kingdom of God, to avoid direct mention of the name of God). Just as Jesus' *person* was introduced in 1:1, his *message* is summarized in the opening verse of this section: "Repent, for the kingdom of heaven is at hand."

Jesus immediately sets about to reconstitute the nation of Israel by calling to him disciples who will share in his proclamation of the kingdom. Note that they are called to become fishers of men. Here the basic ministry-vocation of God's people is recalled and the created purpose of mutual service addressed. God's calling is to ministry—specifically here the calling of men and women into the kingdom. It will be recalled that the commission given in Matthew 28 is to make disciples; so it is important that we understand what Matthew understands by discipleship.

Discipleship in Matthew is a call to attachment to Christ in his calling as the New Israel.[11] Disciples are those who are put in a position to understand the work of Christ, unlike those outside to whom Christ has to speak in parables (and unlike Mark's presentation where the disciples understand very little of what is going on—see Matthew 12:49; 13:36, 51). They are those who really hear what Jesus says and actually do his will; in short, they are those who become like their Master. In Matthew such understanding is the presupposition of faith, which is pictured as trust (6:33). Disciples are those who are empty before God and cleave to his grace (18:1-14) and express Jesus' own solidarity with those in need (25:31-46). So already in Jesus' lifetime they are regarded as fishers of men who are to pray the Lord of the harvest to send forth laborers to join them (9:37, 38).

This section furthermore presents Jesus proclaiming the kingdom by word (chaps. 5-7) and deed (chaps 8, 9) to the crowds. As opposition increases, however, he turns to his disciples and sends them on his mission to the lost sheep of Israel (10:6). Notice that they are given the same authority over disease and spirits as Jesus, so that they might preach and show that the kingdom is at hand and bring peace to those of the house of Israel who believe (v. 13). Why does Jesus limit their travel to Israel? Matthew certainly does not present a good news only for the Jews. We have already noted that the pilgrimage of the Gentiles is illustrated and emphasized early in Matthew (chap. 2), and just after Jesus heals the centurion's servant (8:11) Matthew remembers Jesus' prediction that many will come from distant lands to enjoy God's final celebration with Abraham, Isaac and Jacob. But as Jeremias notes, this is still future (they "will come").[12] Until the cross and resurrection the universal mission of Israel cannot be clear. Meanwhile Jesus' primary purpose is to regather the people of Israel to their true vocation, as the matrix for the re-creation and extension of God's chosen

people.[13] But already it is evident that Gentiles too may
taste the overflow of God's blessing to Israel if they have
faith in Jesus. (Interestingly this point is made at the very
end of this second section in the account of the Canaanite
woman, 15:21-28.)

While the opposition increases (12:14), Matthew identifies Jesus as the servant of the Lord (quoting from Isaiah 41
and 42 in Matthew 12:17-21). And Jesus says clearly that the
kingdom has come in power in his casting out evil spirits
(12:28). In chapter 13 he teaches in parables so that only
those with eyes—that is, his true disciples—will hear and
see (vv. 36-43). This section concludes with Peter's confession in Caesarea Philippi and Jesus' promise that on this
confession or proclamation of faith he would build his
Church (16:18, 19). Again the disciples represent in embryo
the Church that will carry on the program of Christ, the
New Israel.

3. *16:21—28:20*. In spite of the resistance of his disciples to the idea, Jesus begins now to show the necessity of
his suffering and death (16:21, 22). As the beginning of the
first section focused on his person, and the second on his
message, so the third lays out his work. As in Mark, this
death is set in an apocalyptic setting by Jesus' discourse on
the Mount of Olives (chap. 24; cf. Zech. 14). Also like Mark,
signs that are fulfilled in his death and resurrection stand
side by side with those that are still future; all of these are
characteristic of the last days that are now dawning. Even
more clear than in Mark, however, is the stipulation that this
gospel of the kingdom will be preached as a testimony to all
nations before the end will come (v. 14). This is "Jesus' own
promise of what is to take place between his resurrection
and return."[14] Until the victory of divine justice (see 12:20)
God will withhold his final wrath to give room to the calling
of the nations. In that day "God will finally confirm and
make effective the judgment that has already been proclaimed."[15]

Following this, Jesus completes his ministry in Jerusalem by establishing his position as David's son in his trium-

phal entry and his disputations with the Pharisees—as the stone rejected by the builders (21:42) and as David's Lord (22:41-45). He makes clear that his presence continues in the new people that he is forming, so that service to them—even the least of his brethren—will be counted as service to him (25:31-46). Even at his arrest he is pictured as the one who can summon twelve legions of angels (26:53), and he is shown to be innocent in a dream (27:19). But in place of a murderer he dies as the King of the Jews and concludes his role as the New Israel by taking up the lament of God's people on the cross (27:46; cf. Ps. 22:1).

We are now in a position to examine the commission that concludes the gospel (28:18-20). For all the emphases of the Gospel are focused on this command. Jesus directs his disciples, still doubting, to Galilee where he will send them forth as his Church and the agent of his presence in the world (v. 16). He begins by laying claim to the dominion won by his death and resurrection: "All authority in heaven and on earth has been given to me" (v. 18). The note of authority recalls the dominion promised Adam in creation but which has been lost in the fall. Now, however, that dominion has been regained, but to this has been added a dominion over all things in heaven as well. The Lord of the new creation lays claim to the rule of God himself and extends it over this present order. So now "the present is already under the kingly rule of Jesus Christ."[16] "The Divine claim to all things created in heaven and on earth is very concretely Jesus' claim."[17] Behind this claim lies not only the deity of Christ, but also the work of his death and resurrection. For in that act he has reestablished the divine authority over the fallen order and introduced a new kingdom that unites under one banner the powers of heaven and the glories of earth. Now it can be said that there is no purpose or promise of creation that is not fulfilled in principle in the reign of Jesus Christ.

On the strength of this authority the disciples are sent to make disciples. It is important to emphasize that this command rests on the previous announcement. This im-

perative, like all those in the NT, rests on the "great indica-
tive that the time has been fulfilled and the salvation has
come."[18] And as Calvin comments, such authority was surely necessary for one "who commands them to promise eternal life in his name, to reduce the whole world under his
sway, and to publish a doctrine which subdues all pride, and
lays prostrate the whole of the human race." The command,
as has been often observed, is not to "go" but to "make
disciples of all nations." This implies that the meaning of the
missionary calling is the extension of Jesus' own rule in the
world, and that the aim of this preaching is not merely that
people acknowledge his rule but that they follow him as
disciples. Here the context of the OT sense of knowing God
should be recalled. To know Christ here is to acknowledge
his Lordship by following his teachings—that is, to acknowledge his rule in practice. In the context of Matthew the
disciple is the one who hears and obeys the words of the
Lord. Accepting Christ is not merely escaping judgment,
but experiencing his reforming rule, laid out in his teaching,
especially in Matthew 5—7 ("all that I have commanded
you"). The goal of missions here is a permanent reformation
of life by Jesus' words, which is an all-embracing "positive-
critical principle for the life of the world."[19] This goal has not
reached its end until it issues in a people who reflect God's
restorative purposes—who trust God for their needs, care
lovingly for creation and each other, and influence their
communities as salt and light. They will be reflections of
Christ's righteous rule as well as signs of the consummation
of that rule.

    "All nations." Now at last the geographically concen-
trated promise to Israel is universalized. There is no indication here or elsewhere in the NT, however, that Christ's
rule is thereby spiritualized. This point bears emphasis.
With the coming of Christ, the OT truth that "the earth is
the Lord's and the fulness thereof" (Ps. 24:1) is beginning to
be manifested—first in Palestine and then to the ends of the
earth. A new spiritual dimension is added by the resurrec-

tion and Pentecost, but all this is to the end that God's Lordship be *visible* on the earth. Now all creation is to hear and learn of God's new creative work in Christ, so that "God's dominion over all that has been created will yet again shine in unbroken glory."[20] *All nations* may not mean every individual, but people from among all nations. The goal of missions is to find those "who become significant for the existence of their respective nations because the nations now come within reach of the apostolate and its proclamation and receive their concealed center through the Christian community living in their midst."[21]

The baptism in the threefold name of God will be in fire and the Holy Spirit, indicating the judgment and the gift of new life made possible by the death of Christ. The trinitarian formula indicates that the fullness of the Godhead is involved in the work of the new life represented by baptism, which is not causative of salvation but representative of it, "with respect to the salvation brought about by Christ's death and resurrection."[22]

"And lo, I am with you always, to the close of the age." Here the final goal of creation is realized: that God will dwell with his people, even if the reality of his presence is at present hidden from the eyes of many. The Jews believed God was present in the shekinah glory, a presence which in later Jewish history was dependent on a person's being occupied with the law.[23] Now the law is enriched and interpreted by Jesus' own teaching and ministry. And God's own presence is guaranteed in and with the proclamation of the gospel with its goal of renewing lives, communities and even creation. This work which will one day be manifest has begun in mission.

We have referred to this command and promise against the backdrop of God's creative purposes. We could as well show how they are a fulfillment of the promises to Abraham, Moses and David. Here is the first concrete evidence of a holy people and a truly righteous reign, and here too is raised the exciting vision of all creation reflecting this reign.

While it is perfectly clear that this reality is God's own work, there is no doubt that his people will be fully involved in its realization. This is the inner meaning of missions.

Luke: Jesus Offers Salvation to the Lowly

In Luke the central theme is that Jesus fulfills the OT promises and offers salvation to the lowly. While structure seems less important than in the other Gospels, the third Gospel is built around a central journey of Jesus from Galilee to Jerusalem (9:51—19:10). While this motif appears elsewhere, in Luke it emphasizes the Christian life as the "way of the Lord" and salvation history as "a course of events following a schedule of times set by God and directed by God toward all people."[24] But Luke more than any other Gospel features the character of these events and the nature of the salvation Christ brings.

1. The narrative of the birth of Jesus focuses on the fact that the time of salvation promised in the OT has now dawned. We might characterize this revelation in two ways. First, the primary announcement is that salvation has come from heaven and has made its appearance on the earth. Heaven in the Gospel of Luke is "the originating source of all the various authorities operative in God's creation" and in which God conquers the powers of evil.[25] So the primary mission in Luke is that Jesus has crossed the boundary between heaven and earth, bringing salvation. This has the result secondly that earthly and social expectations are overturned. This twofold character can be seen in Mary's hymn of praise (recalling that of Hannah in 1 Samuel 2): "He has shown strength with his arm, he has scattered the proud in the imagination of their hearts" (1:51; cf. vv. 52, 53), and in the announcement to shepherds: "Glory to God in the highest, and on earth peace . . ." (2:14). Simeon sees the salvation which God has prepared for all, a light to the nations (2:29-32), and John's ministry is set in the context of Isaiah 40, which predicts that "all flesh shall see the salvation of God" (3:6). A day of salvation has dawned which is "good news of a great joy which will come to all the people" (2:10).

This salvation has a definite earthly fallout in Luke. We have looked previously at Jesus' programmatic statement of his ministry in Luke 4:18-21 (which is echoed in Jesus' response to John's disciples in 7:22). This period of time is a jubilee that will be characterized by delivering the needy, releasing captives and announcing good news to the poor. The cause of this is a divine visitation which will result in an overturning of usual expectations: the hungry will be filled, the rich sent away empty (1:53). The miracles in Luke are enacted parables that picture the reality of the kingdom to which Jesus points in his teaching. The revelation of the kingdom calls for a particular response pictured in the call of John the Baptist to repentance in chapter 3: "Bear fruits that befit repentance. . . . He who has two coats, let him share with him who has none; and he who has food, let him do likewise" (vv. 8, 11). The continuity with the call of the prophets in the OT is obvious. Repentance is turning to God and acting out the restorative character of the OT law.

2. Coupled with this emphasis on the quality of salvation, Luke emphasizes Jesus' ministry with his disciples, who provide the link between this book and Luke's second volume, the Acts of the Apostles. First Jesus' disciples have left all to follow him (5:11, 28), and are characterized as the poor who will be blessed (6:20-23). "These people all know the sense of futility, incapacity and helplessness" of a situation in which their culture offers them nothing in the way of a future.[26] These are offered salvation which in Luke is characterized by feasting and joy. But almost at once Jesus begins to equip his followers to minister in his name. In chapter 8 he takes them with him on a long tour through cities and villages where they learn about ministry firsthand. In chapter 9 they are sent out for the first time alone, but this must have been only a partial success because afterward they cannot feed the crowd (v. 13) or cast out a demon (v. 40), and they begin to quarrel about who will be greatest (v. 46). In chapter 10 they are sent out again, this time with the very power of Christ, who announces when they return: "I saw Satan fall like lightning from heaven" (v. 18). That is, the

victory you were seeing on earth was the visible counterpart
of a great spiritual victory over the powers of evil in heaven.

Jesus' teaching now features the social fallout of the
dawn of salvation. The rich man who trusts his wealth is a
fool (chap. 12); the poor take the places of the wealthy at the
great banquet (chap. 14); the rich man and Lazarus change
roles (chap. 16); the rich young ruler is told to sell all (chap.
18); and when Zacchaeus promises to restore all he has swin-
dled, Jesus comments, "Today salvation has come to this
house" (19:9). Jesus summarizes these incidents and his
ministry in the following verse: "For the Son of man came to
seek and to save the lost" (v. 10).

But it is the great banquet parable of chapter 14 that is
especially noteworthy, for the banquet theme provides an
important link between OT and NT views of mission. In
Luke 13:29 Jesus predicts that "Men will come from east and
west, and from north and south, and sit at the table in the
kingdom of God." Joachim Jeremias notes that this statement makes it possible for us to interpret all the banquet
parables as pictures of the final enjoyment of salvation in
which all nations may share.[27] We noted that the movement
in mission in the OT was centripetal; that is, the nations
were seen one day to come up to Jerusalem and drink there
the water of life. The goal of such a pilgrimage was that all
creatures would one day enjoy perfect communion with
their Creator. This communion was variously interpreted as
feasting and worship. It is this picture that lies behind the
parable of Luke 14. Now, however, the invitation to those
outside the city is actually being given by Jesus himself. The
pilgrimage is not only a matter of prophecy or isolated types
(cf. the Queen of Sheba); it is now seen to fill up the banquet
house!

As we come to Jesus' command to his disciples to extend this invitation in his name, the relation between the
movement of mission in the OT and that in the NT becomes
clear. The basic direction is still toward communion with
God and the celebration that he is planning. But now this
communion has been realized on the earth in the congrega-

tion of those who gather in his name. So as God's people scatter with the invitation, they carry the reality with them in the form of firstfruits. As they invite them to God's kingdom (which is still to be consummated in the future), they also invite them in to their fellowship where the gifts of the feast are already to be tasted. The banquet, or the foretaste of it, has become a movable feast! Christ's envoys are sent *out* but charged—as we will see when we turn to James—to feature the gift of hospitality, inviting people *in,* as the central virtue of the new community.

3. The suffering and death of Jesus shows to his disciples that he is among them as one who serves (22:27), and that as his disciples they too must share his trials (v. 28) before they will enjoy "eating and drinking at my table in my kingdom" (v. 30). Meanwhile, he gives them their orders for the interim (24:44-53). First he reminds them that all that has happened has fulfilled Moses and the prophets (v. 44). This prophecy, properly understood, indicated that messiahship must be won by suffering and shown in the resurrection (v. 46; cf. v. 26). And it also points out that repentance and forgiveness (which is Luke's expression for conversion[28]) should be preached in his name, beginning in Jerusalem (v. 47). These verses then set the stage for the events of Acts and serve as the link between the two books.

Chapter Thirteen

The Early Church in Mission

Acts: The Work of the Exalted Christ Through the Believers
As Luke featured the fulfillment of OT promises, so Acts
recounts the realization of Jesus' promise to his disciples.
Acts is the continuation of all Jesus "began to do and teach"
(1:1), as this is realized in the life and ministry of the Apostles. The Gospel of Luke concluded with the instructions to
"stay in the city, until you are clothed with power from on
high" (24:49); Acts begins with the pouring out of that power
(chap. 2). Moreover, apostolic preaching in Acts is rooted in
the acts of God in Christ which culminate in the pouring out
of the Holy Spirit, just as Jesus' ministry unfolds in the light
of God's acts in the OT. To indicate the interconnection of
these events and their relation with those of Revelation we
may draw the following diagram.[1]

Gospels	Acts	Revelation
Jesus conquers the spirits/dies and rises	Apostles cast out demons in his name	Final battle with the forces of evil
Jesus' healings and nature miracles	Apostles' healings in Jesus' name/ possessions shared	New heaven and new earth

Jesus' preach-ing invites the lowly to find rest in him	Apostles' tes-timony to Jesus climaxes their preach-ing	Eternal praise to the Lamb that was slain
Jesus calls his followers to repentance and faith in him	Call to faith in Jesus and repentance extended to all the world	God will be all in all

What Jesus began to do and teach inaugurated the kingdom of God, which will be consummated when he returns. But the time between is not merely an interim during which a verbal witness goes out; it is rather an extension of the king-dom that Christ introduced through the power of the Holy Spirit. Christ very clearly promises that because he goes to the Father, greater works than he does will be done by those who believe on him (John 14:12). Such a promise would be merely an embarrassment to the Church were it not for the testimony of the book of Acts.

1. 1:8 gives us the structure and meaning of the entire book. Jesus refuses to answer the disciples' question about the restoration of the kingdom to Israel (remember, this was the focus of all messianic hopes in Judaism). That event has been delayed to make room for the witness the Church will give to Jesus (note that the Apostles, Jesus said, will be "my witnesses"). Verse 8 is less of a command than a promise or a guarantee: you *will receive* power when the Holy Spirit comes upon you, and you *will be* witnesses. The crucial event in mission will be the pouring out of the Holy Spirit. As this event entered the consciousness of the early Church, it gradually came to be thought of as part of the resurrection and exaltation of Christ.[2] The Pentecost experience in Acts is put in obvious parallel with the birth narrative in Luke: the power of salvation is entering the world. The angels an-nounced the significance of Christ's birth in Luke 2:11; Peter

explains the meaning of this heavenly gift in Acts 2. Christ had gathered up all the OT hopes for salvation; now the "gift of the Spirit is the sum total of all that for which Jesus teaches his disciples to pray in the Lord's prayer."[3] The pouring out of the Holy Spirit is the culmination of all previous prophecies.[4] But in making this emphasis Luke by no means places Christ in the background in Acts, for the exaltation of the Lord becomes the key to the present ministries of the Apostles. The power of the Apostles is evidence of Christ's Lordship. As John Calvin put it, Christ ascended "to rule heaven and earth with a more immediate power." He goes on:

> By his ascension he fulfilled what he had promised: that he would be with us even to the end of the world. As his body was raised up above all the heavens, so his power and energy were diffused and spread beyond all the bounds of heaven and earth.[5]

Peter associates the gift of the Holy Spirit with the prophecy in Joel which promises God will pour out his Spirit upon all flesh in the last days. The gift of prophecy which Christ claimed in Nazareth has now been given without reference to social or racial expectations. And it was not to stop with this motley crew of Galileans. Representatives from "every nation under heaven" (v. 5), probably Jews and God-fearers, witnessed this outpouring, and 3,000 of them followed Peter's instructions to repent and be baptized.

2. Consistent with the method of Luke we now are shown the earthly fallout of this heavenly visitation. Acts 2:42-47 describes the life of the new community. There were signs and wonders which issued in an awesome awareness of divine power. Then, as a response to the coming of the Holy Spirit and in fulfillment of Mary's song in Luke 1:53, the believers sold all their possessions and distributed to any that had need. 4:32-35 reemphasizes this aspect and underlines the fact that it was a vital part of the great witness that they gave to the resurrection of Jesus. It was, so to say, the visible fruit of that resurrection. Now to see this as a political

or social program is to miss the point Luke wishes to make. When one follows Christ and receives his power from above, he or she spontaneously shares with others (remember, a disciple in Luke's writings is someone who leaves everything). Moreover, this sharing recalls the abundant provision for all human need that creation offered, and it also harked back to the abundance of the land of Canaan in which all Israel shared equally. At these decisive points God's supply highlighted the fact that his purposes include the meeting of human needs on all levels. Of course, human selfishness intervened here to mar the heavenly fellowship, just as it had done in earlier times (cf. Ananias and Sapphira, chap. 5).

Following immediately is a description of the worship of the new community. They broke bread and praised God, while they enjoyed the apostles' teaching and fellowship (2:42, 46, 47). The note of joy is sounded again, and God continues his work of adding to their number (v. 47). Chapter 3 continues the description of their witness. A lame man at the Temple looks expectantly at Peter and John. They reply that they have no silver or gold (they have left that!), but what they have they will share: the healing power of the Holy Spirit, which is dispensed in Jesus' name. Out of nothing God can create his peace. The resurrection and the coming of the Holy Spirit "awoke in the Early Church a white-hot expectation of immanence."[6]

3. The message of the Apostles may be summed up in a few words.[7] The age of fulfillment had dawned, and the OT prophecies were being fulfilled. By virtue of the resurrection Jesus is now the head of the new Israel, and the Holy Spirit in the Church is the sign of Christ's present power and glory. This reign will soon be consummated by his return. Perhaps Mark 1:14, 15 served as the basic framework for their message (as Dodd believes), but the kingdom for the Apostles now had come to focus on the exalted Jesus.[8] These facts now made it necessary for all people to repent and be baptized and so receive the gifts of forgiveness and the Holy Spirit.

Initially this message spread spontaneously, though

from the beginning one discerns God's active direction. Soon the social program of the Church had become so large that a special organization had to be created for it (chap. 6). But no sooner are these deacons appointed than they begin to act like prophets! Stephen preaches and performs great signs among the people (6:8; chap. 7); Philip explains the gospel to an Ethiopian official. In chapter 8 the believers are scattered and they all begin to preach (v. 4). In chapter 10 Peter is instructed in a dream to take the gospel to Cornelius, and this leads to a new perception of their calling: "To the Gentiles also God has granted repentance unto life" (11:18). By chapter 11 Antioch has become another center of gospel witness, which includes also the sharing of their resources with the Jerusalem church when hard times strike (vv. 29, 30). We consider Paul's great mission journeys below. But here we note that the book ends in Rome, the imperial capital, which Paul intends to make yet another center for the spread of the gospel. The power of the kingdom is reaching to the very centers of power.

Two conclusions emerge from this account. First, the Holy Spirit has been given to equip the Church for its witness, so that one can say of these early Christians: "The essence of being a Christian (is) the activity of mission."[9] But this activity was one in which the whole of their corporate life reflected the character of salvation. Their verbal witness was consistently accompanied by signs of God's presence.

Second, the movement of God's program to the ends of the earth has now begun. Paul, of course, will be the "great prototype for the Church's missionary activity."[10] But we can note here that his sermons in Antioch of Pisidia (chap. 13) and in Athens (chap. 17) give a valuable clue as to the nature of that mission. His presentation of the gospel in these places does not rest on the covenant promises, but on the purposes for which those promises were given: the ends of creation itself. So Paul's appeal to creation and his witness to the Gentiles go together; they show that the promises to Israel have reached their goal. Now the God of creation can be made known among the Gentiles, by Jesus Christ.

Paul: Jesus as the Universal Lord

From the beginning of his life as a Christian Paul lived in mission, his thinking was done as reflection on mission and, ever since, the Church has lived on Paul's missionary epistles. When Paul encounters the risen Christ in Acts 9 he is en route on a mission—to stamp out Christianity. But there on the road to Damascus he sees that the exalted Christ is Lord of the Church he is persecuting. He is blinded by a light and hears a voice addressing him (like Moses in Ex. 3). Seeing Jesus as the risen Lord (1 Cor. 15:8), Paul is forced to conclude that Jesus is vindicated by God. And like Abraham (Gen. 12:1) Paul is immediately given directions: he is to enter the city. There God declares, "He is a chosen instrument of mine to carry my name before the Gentiles and kings and the sons of Israel" (v. 15). Retelling this later, Paul stresses he is sent far away to the Gentiles (Acts 22:21). Here God is fulfilling his great commission.

1. Paul's message was intrinsic to his call: creation has been placed in a new solidarity under the universal Lordship of Christ; now all must believe and obey the gospel. C. H. Dodd sums up this message by saying that in fulfillment of OT prophecies the new age has dawned with the coming of Christ.[11] Christ, born of the seed of David, died according to Scripture to deliver mankind from this present evil age and rose again the third day, vindicated as God's righteous son. This risen and exalted Lord will return as Judge of all men and Savior of all who believe.

References to the kingdom of God, while not altogether missing in Paul (see Eph. 5:5 and Col. 1:13), do not have anything like the centrality they do in the Synoptics. Has this idea been overlooked by Paul? A close study of Paul's theology indicates that the familiar phrase, "in Christ" communicates all that the Gospels mean by the kingdom of God. That is, all the blessings of the kingdom Christ came to preach are given to those who submit to Christ's Lordship. Ridderbos in fact can conclude that "the coming of the Kingdom as the fulfilling eschatological coming of God to the world is the great dynamic principle of Paul's preaching."[12]

The coming of Christ has made possible a new solidarity in righteousness that supersedes that of Adam in sin (cf. Rom. 5:12-21). This reality, which Paul calls a new creation (2 Cor. 5:17), is based on the events of the life of Christ. In Paul we see "that the saving action of God in the Gospels is to be found in the creation of a new people, in a social-historical operation."[13] The present facts that characterize this situation Paul lists as the breaking down of social, ethnic and caste barriers (Eph. 2:14 and Philemon); establishing justice between God and creation by the death of Christ (Rom. 3:21-27); defeat of powers that destroy creation (Col. 1:13; 2:15); and, above all, victory over death (2 Tim. 1:10 and 1 Cor. 15).

The point of Paul's preaching is that these are matters of present fact and that now all mankind must respond to this altered situation. Paul saw as his mission "to bring about the obedience of faith for the sake of (Jesus') name among all the nations" (Rom. 1:5). This call to the nations, however, was still rooted in the promise to Abraham. But now all who believe in Christ become heirs of the promises to Abraham (Gal. 3). As we noted above, Paul's preaching to the Gentiles emphasizes that with the coming of Christ the intention of God for creation has begun to be realized. So the inheritance of God's promises to Israel in Paul's preaching must be placed in the larger context of God's purposes for creation. Paul's preaching certainly enriched the OT promises with deeper insight into the nature of faith as the response of the whole person to God's initiative and the new intimacy this makes possible between the believer and God in Christ (Gal. 2:20). But it would distort Paul's intentions to see that all the former promises are thereby spiritualized. What W. Brueggemann says about land in Pauline literature could be said about many other OT promises: "We cannot therefore deny the central and enduring referent which is land, unless we are to succumb to an otherworldly hermeneutic."[14] The heart is the focus and center of Paul's gospel; it is by no means his exclusive concern. Let us survey some evidence for this fact.

First, it is hard to deny A. N. Wilder's point that the struggle with the powers of evil which Christ fought and won on the cross continues in the Church and will only cease when its Lord comes again.[15] Though the battle is won and the power of victory is ours through the Holy Spirit, the struggle continues as the area of deliverance is extended through the mission of the Church. Christ's deliverance, according to Paul, includes liberation from idols (as in Thessalonica) and from the powers of Satan (in Colossians), as well as from more intimate deities (such as those whose god is their belly!).[16] So when the Christian Church attacks these false authorities in culture and politics, "it is engaged in a strategic attack upon the corrupted structures of society."[17] Paul does not, of course, advocate a direct attack on the Roman authorities, but proclaims a higher authority and a higher righteousness that must sooner or later conflict with wicked and oppressive authorities.

At this point we may offer a comment on the political dimension of Christian witness. It is often argued that the NT offers no support for those who would seek to influence or confront political authorities in the name of Christ. Paul, it is claimed, quite simply urges submission to authorities as ministers of God (Rom. 13:1-7). Before such a far-reaching conclusion is drawn, however, certain aspects of biblical teaching must be borne in mind. First, Paul's comments are perfectly consistent with the OT attitude of openness toward existing institutions. As we noted, the Bible does not provide a divine plan for social and political institutions. Rather, it seeks to work its transforming influence in and through existing structures—challenging them all by the standard of God's justice outlined in the law. Even if the transformation that must (and will!) eventually take place is radical in nature, the biblical way is not to confront these structures directly but to work in them to bring about a more righteous order.

Second, we need to recall that in the teaching of Jesus, he made it very clear that it was his prerogative (not that of government) to set the limits of governmental (and any

other) authority. In the great commission of Matthew, and
now even more clearly in Paul (especially in Ephesians 1), it
is clear that all authorities on earth are subordinated to
Christ's universal Lordship. Part of the message of the gospel, moreover, is the clear announcement of this fact.

Third, both Paul and Jesus make clear that this present
authority must allow, not only the freedom to proclaim the
gospel—which in fact is always assumed and never demanded—but also the freedom to manifest the righteousness of
the new people of God. Paul makes very clear in Galatians
(cf. 5:1) that this freedom is not negotiable. No human power
or institution may be allowed to hinder this. Indeed, Paul's
own death is testimony to this fact. The instructions of Romans 13 then must be read as a statement of the general
divine authorization under which government functions—
"holding no terror for those who do right" (NIV). But it is
inconceivable to suppose that Paul would insist on this principle if governmental authority should conflict with Christ's
Lordship—for then the authorities would clearly no longer
be servants of God.

Socially Paul gave a great deal of attention to the reality
of material and economic sharing among his churches. Probably a major concern of his third missionary journey was his
systematic collection for the poor believers in Jerusalem (see
Rom. 15:22-33). Perhaps because his brethren in Jerusalem
appealed to him (Gal. 2:10) he undertook a major effort of
collecting funds first from the Macedonian churches (who
were themselves far from rich!) and then from the church at
Corinth (2 Cor. 8 and 9). Paul felt it was a matter of simple
justice, reflecting the fact Jesus gave up his riches so that our
poverty might be alleviated (2 Cor. 8:9). From the conclusion of Romans, it is clear that Paul felt this represented the
possibility of universal sharing between nations manifesting
the new solidarity in Christ, and that would, he hoped,
make it possible for him to extend his work soon into
Spain.[18] Interestingly the closest parallel in Judaism is the
Temple tax sent yearly from dispersed Jews to Jerusalem.
Here, Paul may be implying, is the new Temple of God

conducting its services (Eph. 2:21). Again Paul does not attack wealth directly but raises a new standard of sharing that suggests a wholly new attitude toward riches.

Finally, when the slave Onesimus is sent back to his master Philemon after he had become a believer, Paul says simply, receive him "no longer as a slave but more than a slave, as a beloved brother" (Philemon 16). Here Paul shows his continuity with the OT law wherein institutions are accepted and transformed in the light of God's redemptive love. God's method of change is not by violence or social engineering, but it is just as surely subversive. For slavery as an institution would not long survive the influence of these simple instructions. The universal solidarity that believers share in Christ has cast its shadow even here.

2. Mission then was a natural consequence of the new solidarity that Christ came to realize. Paul Minear describes Paul's work in these terms:

> The unity of the Church can be seen as embodied in the activity of glorifying God with one voice (Rom. 15:6) and the mission of the Church can be described as the method by which men, through enabling others to glorify God for his mercy (15:9), participate in the multiplication of thanksgiving to the glory of God (II Cor. 4:15).[19]

The Jewish people, in Paul's mind, had the privilege of first hearing the gospel. Even though he knew himself sent to the Gentiles, he often went first to the synagogue. The rejection of the gospel by his own people was one of Paul's most troubling theological problems, and he discusses the matter in Romans 9—11. Oscar Cullmann believes these chapters are simply commentary on Mark 13:10. Since all people must now have the chance to hear, and the Jews have neglected their opportunity, the word will now go to the Gentiles before the Jews will enter the kingdom.[20] "A direct route to Christ is made for the nations through Israel's stepping aside."[21] Once again God will use the exile of his people for the benefit of the nations. But at the same time Paul argues that God has not rejected his people, for, as in the OT, there is now a righteous remnant (11:5), who represent the olive tree (11:17, 18). God has not forgotten his promises to his people, and at the end he will again gather them to himself (Rom. 11:26, which quotes Isa. 59:20, 21). The few are a pledge of the salvation of all. But Paul's mission rests on the fact that Christ's Lordship is universal, and so G. Bornkamm can well say, "The apostle's preaching before Jews cannot be separated, either materially or historically, from his preaching before Gentiles."[22]

Ideally a study of Paul's mission should proceed by a study of each of his epistles in their context. This is not possible for us, but we may make comments on two of his major letters.

1. *Ephesians* draws out the implications of the fact that God has now purposed to unite everything in heaven and on earth in Christ (1:10). We who acknowledge his Lordship already experience this reign as a present fact—as "sons and daughters" (1:5). For us, racial barriers no longer exist (chap. 2). Paul's ministry of the gospel then includes the making known of the plan hidden by God: "that through the church the manifold wisdom of God might now be made known to the principalities and powers" (3:10). Chapters 4—6 go on to outline the concrete shape of the new reality in which we participate: a community where people patiently accept one another, speak the truth (as members of one another), are pure in their behavior, subject to one another and strengthened to fight the powers of evil. Here the OT law is enriched and personalized, recalling the radical reinterpretation of Christ in the sermon on the mount; it is deepened but not abrogated.

2. *Romans*. Paul is writing to several congregations in Rome, each reflecting various stages of maturity, because he wishes to make of them a loyal base of operation (as Jerusalem and Antioch had been before) for a further thrust of missions into Spain.[23] The last thing on his agenda before coming to visit Rome was the delivery of the collection to the church in Jerusalem, and it is obvious that both this collec-

tion and the letter play a crucial role in his missionary planning. The theology of Romans is written then as a reflection on his missionary strategy. God's salvation is universal, as universal as human sinfulness. But how can one call on one they do not know (10:12-14)? Remember, the goal of missionary proclamation is the obedience of faith (Rom. 1:5); but this response necessitates Paul's mission. So he hopes to go to Rome to be sped on his way to Spain (15:23, 24). God had another trip to Rome in mind for Paul, under Roman guard, but this treatise stands as a reminder that the point of the theological reflections of Romans, if we are true to its author's intention, is that the gospel be preached to the ends of the earth!

James: The Voice of a Prophet in the Early Church

As the Church spread, there arose the necessity for prophets to call it back to its original vocation when it had grown cold. As in the OT, the NT prophet reminded the people of their covenant obligations to know the Lord: that is, to reflect the loyalty to the new covenant by her corporate life in the world.

James echoes this prophetic voice not only of the OT but of Jesus himself. The prophetic critique of Jesus (especially as seen in Matthew) is overheard in James as well.[24] In Matthew 9:9-13, for example, Christ reminds the Pharisees (quoting Hosea 6:6) that God desires the merciful acceptance of the weak and not only ritual obedience. Christ did not reject the external law, but wished merely to show that the ethical sphere is "the indispensable foundation of the ritual sphere."[25] Then by his frequent references to banquets and feasts (Matt. 8:11), Christ indicated that the disciples' vocation would include inviting the lonely and hungry to fellowship with God's people. In Luke 14:12-24, in fact, it is the poor and outcast who take the place of the rich and self-satisfied as God's honored guests.

James 2 reflects the time in Jerusalem when respect of persons had replaced the initial sharing of Acts 2 and 4. Jesus accepted sinners, but the Church had come to accept the rich—in direct violation of the demands of mercy (v. 13). This reality James goes on to describe (in vv. 14-16) as the spontaneous hospitality toward those in need which reflects God's own supply of human need. James then reminds the church at Jerusalem that their community is to be a sign of the kingdom of God and the place where its powers are at work.

John: The Church Demonstrates the Reality of the Incarnation

John's Gospel studied in relation to the epistles of John gives us the unique opportunity of seeing how the message of the gospel is meant to apply to the life of a particular congregation as it seeks to witness to its faith. Both are written late in the first century and represent a later stage in the Church's reflection on the gospel (perhaps at the time when Christians had been put out of the synagogue[26]). The purpose of the Gospel is to stimulate faith in Christ (John 20:31), while the epistles encourage a faithful witness to Christ (1 John 4:1-3) so as to extend the fellowship (1:3). This witness is a drama in three stages:

1. Jesus has revealed the glory of God in the world. The basic movement in John's Gospel is from God to earth: Jesus is sent into the world to reveal light (or eternal life or salvation: 3:17; 17:18; and 1 John 4:14). John begins by presenting Christ as the *logos* or mediator of creation. In John, Christ reveals the inner meaning and goal of creation: the communion of love between Creator and creature. "Christian theology has unfolded in the doctrine of creation the universal relevance of God's love as revealed in Jesus."[27] The focus of this revelation is the person of Jesus, in whom God's glory "tabernacles" within his creation (1:14).

In John, Jesus' teaching and work draw attention to his person. The parables in the Synoptics are replaced in John by the famous "I am" statements (which as Miranda notes are often quoted directly from Isaiah[28]). This substitution incidentally may help us understand the ultimate purpose of the parables in uncovering Jesus' self-consciousness. Only seven miracles appear in John, and each serves as the basis for a long interpretive summary underlining the point of the miracle as a sign of Jesus' work. "Side by side, the words and the miraculous deed gave expression to God's entrance into time."[29] These miracles are "signs" or works (John's unique term for them), to be seen in continuity with the works of God in the OT: creation, the Exodus, the Exile—symbolic acts which realize God's purposes (cf. John 12:37 and Num. 14:11[30]). Jesus' final work is the cross. In a unique way his death is his own work (10:18). He is not passive as in Mark; he is the one who decides "It is finished" (19:30). The cross then is the place where Jesus finishes the work God gave him to do and thus glorifies God on the earth (17:1-5). But note that the words and works go together in John (indeed the words are also works: 14:10). Both have made eternal life available to mankind on the earth in the present (and not at the end of the age—4:14; 3:18, 19; 17:3). Jesus has brought eternal life to earth, and he gives it freely (5:21; 11:25).

2. The reality of eternal life is mediated to God's people by the coming of the Paraclete (the Holy Spirit). When the Word became flesh, "the world of spirit has been brought into the world of time, and this penetration has resulted in a transformation."[31] In chapters 14—16 Jesus explains that though he must go away, he will send the Holy Spirit to them (16:7). His work, like that of Jesus, will be world-embracing (as it is the work of God creating the new order): "When he comes, he will convince the world concerning sin and righteousness and judgment" (16:8; see the full trinitarian involvement in vv. 14, 15).

The presence of this Comforter will become the basis of Jesus' sending his disciples into the world. His followers qualify on the basis of their belief that God has sent Jesus (17:8 and 1 John 4:2, 14). To these, Jesus has given the word which sanctifies them (John 17:15, 17). Now note carefully what Jesus promises these renewed disciples. Because of this intimacy between Jesus and his followers, they will be able to do even greater works than he does (14:12), for they will ask the Father whatever they wish in Jesus' name

(14:13). This in turn forms the basis of Jesus' purposes for his disciples. Interestingly, the commission Jesus gives his disciples first appears as a prayer to the Father (17:18) and is repeated in 20:21: "Peace be with you. As the Father has sent me, even so I send you."

The Paraclete then becomes the link between Jesus' work on earth and his work in the Church. This is clear in John's use of the temple image. At the cleansing of the Temple Jesus says he can rebuild this temple in three days; but he is speaking, John says, of his body (2:19, 21). At the Feast of Tabernacles—celebrated in the Temple by pouring out water in front of the altar—he stands up and proclaims that anyone who comes to him and drinks, "Out of his heart shall flow rivers of living water" (7:38). Christ probably refers here to Ezekiel's vision of the Temple wherein water flowed by the threshold (Ezek. 47:1, 2), and he anticipates John's vision of the water flowing from the throne of God in heaven (Rev. 22:1, 2). But in the fourth Gospel this water refers to the Holy Spirit who would be given to the believer (7:39). In the Holy Spirit, the believer enjoys the presence of Christ himself and tastes the water of eternal life. But what will this mean for our life in the world?

3. The incarnation is continued in the witness of the believing community (1 John). The one who believes in Jesus, for John, has a unique role to play as witness (John 3:32 and 8:13). In 1 John the witness fulfills Jesus' prayer in John 17 by communicating life to the world, for the believers' witness creates a wider fellowship (1:1-4). In the believer "in fellowship with all believers and with the Father and the Son, the divine redemption has its locus."[32] But in 1 John it is very clear that the authenticity of the witness does not rest on a purely verbal witness (4:2, 3), but in showing to the world the greater power dwelling in the believer (4:4). This is summarized in 3:23 as loving, which must be in deed as well as word (see 3:17, 18). The real mark of truth in 1 John is the confession of the incarnation, which is marked by mutual fellowship, walking in the light, forgiving sins, enjoying victory over the devil and keeping Christ's commandments.

True confession is showing the visible reality of Christ's love incarnated in the community to the extent of laying down one's life for a brother (3:16[33]). This is the confession that Jesus has come in the flesh. The problem facing the Church in John's time was how one can show which spirits were from God and which were not. The answer lies in the fact that the reality that voices the confession also manifests the life.[34]

So the key to John is the incarnation. But the reality of the incarnation is to be reflected in the witness of the Church. The following verses indicate this progression:

John 1:12, 14	John 16:16	1 John 4:2
The Word dwells among us.	Christ will go and come again.	Every spirit confessing that Jesus has come in the flesh is from God (Jesus present in the Spirit!).

So visible confession belongs intrinsically to the nature of the Church and grows out of her abiding in Christ (John 15:1-11). Moreover, it includes all the works of Christ (and greater!) within its purview. The testimony-work of the disciples grows out of the testimony-work of Christ. The way to communicate life is by making the life-giving sharing of ourselves as central to our lives as it was to Christ's.[35]

Summary: The Church Is the Locus and Agent of the Kingdom in the World
The expansion of God's promise has come to focus on the Church which Christ founded. In Luke and Acts, this is the place where the heavenly powers which Christ revealed become visible on the earth. In Paul's thought, the Church is the place where the new unity of all things in heaven and on earth comes to historical expression. The Church is also the

community where the royal law of love reigns (James) and where the reality of the incarnation becomes evident (John). But if the Church is the center of God's activity in this period of history, it does not comprise the whole of that activity. For the kingdom of God is larger than the Church. The powers of the kingdom have created the Church, and the Church witnesses by life and word to the kingdom as its agent.[36] But the Church is still a sign that one day God's glory will cover the earth as the waters cover the sea. So the kingdom is both the foundation of the Church and the goal of the world. And mission is the means by which the future of the kingdom moves the world toward its final salvation.[37]

Looking back, we can say that in the Church the creative purposes of God for the world are beginning to be realized. While still existing amidst the suffering of the fallen order, she exhibits, by virtue of her identification with Christ, the presence of the new creation. Amidst the form of this world which is passing away, a seed has been planted in the world that will grow to perfection and will feature all that is valuable from this created order. This connection of the Church with creation featured prominently in the early Church. In the Shepherd of Hermas (mid-second century) Hermas learns that the aged woman he sees is the Church and asks why she is so old: "Because she was created before all things," answers his guide; "therefore she is aged; and for her sake the world was framed" (V. 2. iv).

Looking ahead, the Church is the sign of the new order, the place where God's final purposes for the world and its people may be glimpsed. It lives in the light cast by the resurrection of Christ. Christ was raised that we too might "walk in newness of life" (Rom. 6:4). As we have noted often, though God's act is the all-important factor, God's action is a summons (the phrase is from Stauffer[38]). As God has called the needy to himself in Christ, so we are called to echo and reflect that call. The call of the Church in mission is not a sign that the end has come, but that the last days have arrived. It is a sign "of the time and history that still endured and that had been determined in relation to the end."[39]

While we understand that the meaning of this delay is mission, the concrete expression of God's mercy, we must know more about the end that is coming if our lives are to have a particular contour during this period. One needs a goal in order to have direction.

Act Five

The Consummation

The brain is a history library that has run in the future tense. Almost all our thinking activity is directed towards dealing with the future since all actions taken are directed towards bringing about an effect which is not yet present.

Edward de Bono

Chapter Fourteen

The End and Goal of Creation: The New Heaven and New Earth

Introduction

We noticed that creation and the whole of biblical history has the special character of promise. People who believe in God are tied in a unique way to the future.[1] Because it is God that fashions the end, he must finally create something which will perfectly correspond to him, in which he can come to rest. At the same time each fulfillment of the promise, though partial, liberates a still greater hope.[2] Already our study has shown that the promise threatens to spill over history. Christ could hardly avoid pulling back the curtain of space and time and revealing undreamed of horizons. Though now at times things seem dark, we live in the period of the highest hopes because we live under the final promise: the resurrection of Jesus and the Pentecost miracle. As the horizon of the future opens to us, the scope of our responsibility to this world increases and the breadth of our mission increases.

For perspective on these things we turn to John's revelation on Patmos. There all the strands of Scripture are woven together in a final complex of images. The Book of Revelation follows a familiar literary technique called *inclusio* wherein "the final episode in the story repeats and balances the first."[3] N. A. Dahl has pointed out that a common theme of images of the last things in the NT is that "the end will bring the final realization of what from the beginning was the will of God the creator, who is himself the first and the last."[4] While expanding and enlarging the promise of creation, the new creation when consummated will realize all that God wished to accomplish in his original work.

The idea of *inclusio* may also give us a hint as to how we may understand the unity of Scripture. As the end sums up the whole, so it uncovers its intrinsic unity. The play is only seen as a unity when the final curtain comes down. But in the Book of Revelation the unity is only suggested, not explained. For the simple fact is that our minds and imaginations cannot grasp what the end will really be like (cf. 1 Cor. 2:9, which quotes Isa. 64:4). And in Revelation we should be prepared for the fact that the continuity with previous Scripture is a matter of images rather than concepts. The images of Revelation—the horsemen, the dragon, the New Jerusalem and the river of life—have impact and meaning on several levels, but they cannot always be neatly tied down. We must allow them to master us as they open up God's future. Let us then turn to this "great drama of poetical conciseness"[5] and reflect on how our mission may be shaped by its reality.

A Vision of God

Revelation begins and ends with a vision of God (chaps. 1, 21, 22); the central section of judgment begins with a vision of God in heaven (chaps. 4, 5); and more hymns of praise and doxology are scattered through its visions than any book in the Bible except the Psalms. The visions are given on "the Lord's day" (1:10), indicating that the context of the visions is one of worship. The presence of God is the controlling factor of the dramatic action and full communion with God the goal. In the first vision Christ is presented as redeemer (1:5-7) and as ruling Lord with all the attributes of God walking amidst the churches (1:9-20). Central is the doxology of verses 5b-7 which quotes Exodus 19:6; what God promised to do in the Exodus, Jesus has done by his redeeming death.

The visions of chapter 4 and 5 are really the controlling

visions of the book. John is taken to heaven and the throne of
God with its rainbows, jasper, thunder and lightning (cf. Ex.
24:10, 16-18) and four living creatures (Ezek. 1:4-14). But
the view of God in these chapters is not static; he is a speaking, acting God who reveals himself on the earth and receives the worship of the heavenly hosts. The action centers
around the scroll which no one on earth or in heaven is able
to open. When one of the elders announces that the Lion of
Judah "has conquered" and therefore can open the scroll,
the twenty-four elders sing a new song to the Lamb, who
alone is worthy to reveal the secrets of the future. As M.
Rissi points out,[6] the expression "has conquered" provides
the key not only for this vision but the entire book (5:5). For
the decisive encounter in the Book of Revelation has already
occurred in the death and resurrection of Christ; the glories
of the consummation in one sense are but the unveiling of
the victory that Christ has already won. Again a doxology
focuses the praise (5:9, 10), paralleling that in chapter 1
except for one crucial addition: "and they shall reign on
earth" (5:10b). Here the political dimension of the consummation is specially underlined.

A Vision of the Church

Revelation was probably written during the persecution of
the Church under the Roman Emperor Domitian (A.D. 81-
96). So the immediate purpose of the book was to present a
prophetic interpretation of their persecutions and their witness from the viewpoint of the end.[7] It was to provide comfort and assurance in the midst of suffering (1:9; 6:10, 11).
Chapters 2 and 3 introduce the Church and provide what
Ms. Fiorenza calls the "ecclesial framework" for the book.[8]
But note that in spite of the fact that the Church is suffering,
Christ still holds her responsible. The response required of
her, in fact, picks up themes common throughout Scripture:
she must repent of evil, be faithful unto death, keep his
word, not become self-sufficient in riches. But the one who
conquers and keeps his works (2:26) is promised power over
the nations to rule with a rod of iron (2:26, 27, recalling Ps.

2:9); to be made a pillar in the Temple of God (3:12); and a place on the throne of God (3:21). Again the note of dominion over the earth and the nations is sounded. Though weak and suffering, God's people are promised a share in God's own rule. Meanwhile, their witness lies in keeping his word and his works.

A Vision of Judgment on the Earth and Its Peoples

1. Following the vision of God in heaven (chaps. 4, 5), a time of troubles in human society and in nature is portrayed in the seven seals. At the outset, however, John sees a rider on a white horse going out conquering and to conquer (6:2). Reiterating the promise of Mark 13:10, this rider pictures the proclamation of the gospel of Christ in all the world.[9] The Church will suffer with the world, but the standard she raises controls this period of struggle. The little scroll (chap. 10) gives the prophetic interpretation of the community's life during these trials, which is further explained in 14:6-20.[10] There again the assurance of the proclamation of the gospel (v. 6) is given:

> Fear God and give him glory, for the hour of his judgment has come; and worship him who made heaven and earth, the sea and the fountains of water. (v. 7)

The gospel, as we have noted, announces the judgment of the Creator God even as it expresses his mercy. But the community must also be on guard, for the danger of apostasy is real (v. 9).

Meanwhile, God will reinforce the preaching of the gospel by portents and calamities on the earth. While the judgment that begins is real and well deserved, in the beginning it is limited (to one-third of the earth or its people), to show God's desire that people repent of their wickedness. As in the plagues in Egypt, God is using natural catastrophes to urge people to repent (chap. 8). Following this, he uses even the demonic hosts to bring judgment upon the earth (chap. 9). In spite of these signs of God's wrath the refrain is heard: "The rest of mankind . . . did not repent of the works of their hands" (9:20). Despite the hope represented by the gospel and the promise of judgment, many do not repent.

These preliminary troubles lead to a final confrontation between the forces of evil and Christ at his appearing (chap. 19). While there is much struggle and suffering here, it is possible to overestimate the element of battle. Chapter 17, for example, begins with an invitation to see the judgment (not battle) of the great harlot who has committed fornication with the kings of the earth. As we have observed, the victory of Christ in the past (5:5) controls all the visions of the book, so that the final encounter is more a revelation of that victory rather than another triumph.[11] Though it is true the enemy makes great preparations for battle and the armies of heaven appear with Christ, when Christ appears in 19:11 there is no battle—the enemy forces simply break down. Nevertheless, the wrath of God is fully expressed: the nations are struck with a rod of iron and Christ treads out the winepress of the fury of the wrath of God the Almighty (19:15, quoting Ps. 2:9 and Isa. 63:3). Notice however, as in 6:2, 19:11 pictures Christ coming on a white horse, indicating that in the preaching of the gospel the final judgment is anticipated. In the word of the gospel the coming Lord appears to heal and to forgive.

2. We are ready, then, to outline in more detail than was possible before the meaning of this last period of time. The overriding question of Revelation is the cry of the saints: why must we still suffer (6:10, 11)? The answer given is, they must rest "a little longer" until their number is complete— that is, until the preaching of the gospel has borne its fruit and all the places at the banquet are filled.

This period of time then reveals the *mercy of God,* a mercy that is expressed clearly in the call of the gospel. When Peter deals with the scoffers who ask why the coming of the Lord is delayed, he answers: "The Lord is not slow about his promise as some count slowness, but is forbearing toward you, not wishing that any should perish" (2 Pet. 3:9). There has been much discussion about what it is that re-

strains, or detains, the Antichrist in 2 Thessalonians 2:6. It is
possible (as H. Berkhof and John Calvin believe) that this is
the preaching of the gospel. This verse then would be understood in terms of Mark 13:10; the gospel must first be
preached in all the world before the end comes.

But this must not be thought of only in negative terms,
as though evangelism was only a matter of snatching brands
from the fire. This period also expresses the *grace of God*,
for it is a time in which the power of the resurrection is
active. Christ was raised, Paul reminds us, so that "we too
might walk in newness of life" (Rom. 6:4). As the Sabbath
and Canaan were in the OT pointers to the promised future,
so now the Church is the "sign" of Christ's reign and its
activities a pointer to his victory. As John Calvin explained
this: "by constraining men to obey him in the preaching of
the Gospel, (Christ) establishes his throne on the earth."[12]
In Revelation this positive rule is evident as God preserves
his people (12:6, 14) and the earth for their sake (7:3; 9:4, 5).

Finally, however, this period is a time of gathering
opposition to Christ's reign. Scripture teaches that the end
time will be specifically marked by countersigns—suffering,
apostasy and catastrophes—all of which come to focus in the
image of the Antichrist. But note that it is of necessity the
appearance of the Christian hope that brings out competitive
doctrines of salvation; it is the presence of righteousness that
stimulates persecution.[13] Finally the Beast actually comes
to the point of taking the place of God (Rev. 13). Notice,
however, that whatever we make of these images, Revelation makes it clear that this struggle will inevitably have a
political dimension. In Revelation this obviously represented the Roman Empire. So "only when Satan and the
concrete representation of his power, the Roman Empire,
no longer rule on earth is final salvation possible."[14] Richard
Mouw adds, "The coming of the kingdom will require an
official acknowledgement on the part of human institutional
authorities of the sovereign rule of God."[15] Only then will
his people reign on the earth (5:10). Before we turn to this
final rule, however, we must inquire into the future of this
created order.

3. We have stressed throughout our study that the created order is the basic context for our service to God. What will the final judgment mean for the earth? Will it simply be destroyed, or is there continuity with the new creation God will create? To answer these questions we must return to two crucial passages that consider this elsewhere in the NT.

2 Peter 3:10, 11. The context of these verses is Peter's warning about the character of the last days. Scoffers will use the very constancy of the created order as an argument against God's promises (v. 4). They forget two things, says Peter. First, the same God that created the world by his word has stored it up for fire "being kept until the day of judgment and destruction of ungodly men" (v. 7). Second, the very delay expresses the mercy of God, who desires all men to repent (v. 9). But the day of the Lord—that is, the day of judgment—will come. To describe this, Peter uses language from the apocalyptic tradition and the OT (Ex. 15; Ps. 18, 89) and the Olivet Discourse; that is, he uses fantastic images to express a reality that transcends our ordinary powers of expression. There will be a cosmic catastrophe in which heaven will "disappear in a roar of flames,"[16] and the elements will be dissolved. The following verse describes the outcome of the judgment. Older translations have elected the Greek reading consistent with previous verses but with less manuscript support: "the earth and the works that are upon it will be *burned up*" (v. 10, RSV). The newer translations follow the better manuscripts and read for "burned" "discovered" or "laid bare" (cf. NIV, NEB). This reading implies that the process of judgment is such that the essential qualities of the earth will be preserved, while what is evil will be destroyed. This is consistent with the use of fire in Scripture as a purifying rather than a destructive element (cf. 1 Cor. 3:12-15 *et al*). What is envisioned here, then, is a judgment through fire, a kind of cosmic death out of which emerges a renewed earth.

Romans 8:19-21. Support for this line of thinking is found in the second passage, from Romans, where the strongest NT evidence appears that the earth is destined to share in the redemption of God's people. The context in chapter 8 is the life that is promised to the one who is righteous by faith and the complete liberation promised in the gospel (v. 2). Verses 17-30 mark a transition from obedience to the hope that belongs to one possessed by the Holy Spirit and who is thus a joint-heir with Christ. Our verses then emphasize that creation itself waits with a "neck-straining expectancy" for the revealing of something that is now hidden from view.[17] This hidden reality is the completion of redemption associated in verse 23b with the resurrection. Creation was subjected to futility at the time of the curse (Gen. 3:17-19), obviously by God himself, and thus has failed to reach the goal set for it (explained in v. 21 as "bondage to decay"). Despite decay, however, there is hope that the final purposes of God for the earth will triumph. But this cannot happen until mankind is able to play its proper role of having dominion: "the glorious liberty of the children of God" (v. 19b). When that dominion is restored (as Revelation so amply assures us it will be), then creation itself will be liberated. "Paul sees the future glory of believers not by itself but accompanied by the glorious liberation of the whole subhuman creation."[18] Meanwhile, creation groans and waits expectantly, with a hope that focuses on those who already live righteously!

A Vision of the End of History

The end will surely come, but Revelation makes it clear that this is no predetermined process that is working like a kind of fate. It will be the personal decision of God, and it will take into account the activities of his people. The preaching of the gospel is already a sign that the end approaches. As previously in Scripture, moreover, God remains open to the cry of his people. One of the earliest prayers in the Church was the prayer, "May our Lord come," a prayer which closes the Book of Revelation (22:20). So it is that though God delays his coming because of his mercy, he may shorten the time for the sake of his people who cry out to him for deliver-

ance (cf. Luke 18:7). The last days unfold in the context of a
dialogue between God and his people.

Revelation pictures this end of history in two separate
stages, the first described in chapter 20, the second in chapters 21, 22. The first stage is the establishment of Christ's
kingdom on the earth, pictured in Revelation 20:1-10 and
usually called the millennium. The background of this picture lies in the OT sabbath rest for the land and the Jewish
messianic kingdom which precedes the end of all things.
(Klein believes Paul may have this in mind in 1 Corinthians
15:24.[19]) It is also the fulfillment of the Christians' prayer
that God's will be done on earth as it is in heaven and of
Christ's promise that the meek (his followers) shall inherit
the earth.

The millennium is an image of the perfection and completion of God's created work, what might be called the
sabbath week of creation. "The kingdom of Christ (is) the
sabbath week of history so fulfilling the type of the kingdom
in the sabbath of creation."[20] During this period the powers
of evil will objectively cease to exist in the world, and the
power of the resurrection will break out in the whole of
human existence.[21] Finally, in fulfillment of Revelation 5:10,
God's people will reign with Christ on the earth. At last, in
fulfillment of the promises to Adam and to David, final
dominion will be realized. As M. Rissi says, the dominion
belonging to the Church by virtue of Christ's work will be
revealed, "their secret nature will be revealed."[22] The mil-
lennial kingdom is an image of great power and meaning even
if we cannot describe it exactly. The number of years—
1,000—may stand for a perfectly long period of time, a week
of years. But it marks the perfect triumph of Christ's kingdom on earth, the perfection of creation, the link between
this world and the next.

The second and final period of the end is called a new
saving act in which everything will be made new (21:5). This
represents the goal of God's creative and redemptive work
and is described by John as a heavenly city coming down out

of heaven. But note that while it is clearly a new creative work (21:1) there is a continuity implied with the present order. Consider the following:

First the NT makes it plain that God's people are already, in the last days, citizens of heaven (Heb. 12:22; Phil. 3:20; and Gal. 4:26). Revelation continues this idea, speaking of God's people as dwelling in heaven even while they suffer on the earth (13:6; 5:9-13; 12:12). That is, because of the gift of the Holy Spirit and the reality of the resurrection-life of Christ, God's people have tasted already the reality of the age to come.

While the judgment spoken of in chapter 21 (and in 2 Peter 3) will be complete and final, the Scriptures imply that it brings with it the perfection and salvation of all that is good and perfect. We have noticed all the way through our study that God's work of judgment has another side of renewal and salvation. It is clear that this will be true of God's final judgment as well. The final judgment is pictured in Revelation as primarily a destruction of death and Satan—those things which threaten creation—rather than of creation itself. As G. R. Beasley-Murray comments: "There is not a line of John's description of the city of God which is not capable of realization in measure within history, although its perfect expression requires the transcendent order as John makes plain."[23] The dimensions of the city may transcend space and time as we know it, but Revelation pictures this as the perfecting rather than the destruction of created structures. Indeed, the very fact that John uses elements from our experience to describe what is in one sense indescribable indicates that the New Jerusalem gives to this order a higher meaning. John's vision, Paul Minear says, "gives to man's existence within space and time a final and indestructible meaning."[24]

Finally continuity is confirmed by the fact that twice John mentions that all the glory of the nations will be brought into the New Jerusalem (21:24, 26). There will be a continuing battle between the values of Jerusalem and those of Babylon in these last days. While we cannot always identify which nation in history belongs where, we can say on the basis of Revelation that what is of Jerusalem will find a place in the new creation, while what is of Babylon will be destroyed. (Mouw[25] goes on to argue that in some sense historically developed institutions will be "received" into the kingdom of God; cf. Revelation 22:2, 3.) For the NT makes it plain that our works will follow us. So we can invest ourselves in the seemingly hopeless work of making our society and its institutions more just because by faith we see through them to the heavenly Jerusalem.

As the goal God has for his people is one in which the structures and environment reflect the loving communion among persons that will prevail, so we must do more than encourage individual human development. God desires a place where people may be truly human and reflect him. So our witness must tend to change places as well as people. We insist on this precisely because God will one day transform both into his likeness. Such a faith, Míguez-Bonino believes, "makes it possible for the Christian to invest his life historically in the building of a temporary and imperfect order with the certainty that neither he nor his efforts is meaningless or lost."[26]

The image of the New Jerusalem is the climactic event in the biblical drama. It brings together all the prophetic strands of Scripture and unites God, his people and heaven and earth into a single glorious unity. The center of the vision is the fact that God's dwelling is with man. Then the communion of biblical religion is perfected. There will be no more Temple, and the light of his presence will be manifested—there will be no sun. God will at that time completely reveal himself, and his presence will be the determining reality of the new city. At the same time, this is the place of God's people. There is an interesting ambiguity to the heavenly city: it is city and it is a people (just as Jerusalem is often used both as a city and as a people). Now the people of God who doubted and were wavering in chapters 2 and 3, who suffered in chapter 6 are perfected and glorified (21:3, 4). They are called a people, a son (21:7), and yet they are nations (22:2). They will experience no suffering (21:4) and will know complete satisfaction of their needs:

> They shall hunger no more,
> Neither thirst any more;
> The sun shall not strike them,
> nor any scorching heat.
> For the Lamb in the midst of the throne
>   will be their shepherd. (7:16, 17)

The New Jerusalem represents finally a new and perfected created order, a "resurrection" of the earth that will match that of the body. But this creation—perfect in splendor and righteousness and radiant in beauty and life—will link heaven and earth in one reality. The river of life flowing from the throne of God "symbolizes the fulness of life-powers which flow through paradise,"[27] but also reminds us of the waters in Eden (Gen. 2:10) and the river in Ezekiel's vision of the temple (Ezek. 47:1, 12). This home for God and man will be the ultimate source and locus of all creativity, the home for all the glory of the nations. But alas, there are walls; John goes to great length to describe them in 21:9-21. Though they reflect the beauty that is inside and though their gates are always open (as the way to God has always been open throughout Scripture), there is an outside and an inside: for "nothing unclean shall enter it, nor any one who practices abomination or falsehood, but only those who are written in the Lamb's book of life" (21:27).

This is the future that even now determines and shapes our present. For it is to this future order that we belong, and to which we are meant to point with every fibre of life and work.

Chapter Fifteen

Epilogue

We have surveyed the biblical perspective of God's program, and we must now return to our original question: does the hope that God holds out for the world have any relation to the human hopes that seethe around us? Is there any way that our work on these human hopes relates to God's mission? But before we seek to answer these questions we must clear away some misconceptions that have influenced our thinking about mission. Perhaps our biblical survey will have equipped us to spot areas where we need to do some rethinking of the Church's missionary vision.

Matter and Spirit

The influence of the Greek dichotomy of matter and spirit was felt early in the Church's reflection upon Scripture. This was best illustrated by the second-century Marcion, who insisted the wrathful God of the OT had nothing in common with the NT God of love. While the Church rejected such extreme views, there has been the tendency to believe that the spiritual message of the NT has superseded the more material emphasis of the OT. Professor Jeremias, for example, insists, "In the sayings of Jesus, the conception of the kingdom is stripped not only of all nationalistic features but also of all materialistic features."[1] Matthew says that the meek shall inherit the earth, and W. D. Davies believes "It is the kingdom of God that transcends geography as Jesus proclaims it, not the geographically concentrated 'promise' of the Old Testament."[2] Davies concludes his important study of these things by saying: "For the holiness of place, Christianity has fundamentally, though not consistently, substituted the holiness of the Person: it has Christified holy space."[3] What are we to make of this new emphasis? Has creation now no role to play in the manifestation of the kingdom?

One can hardly deny that the NT focuses on the heart of the individual person and brings about a new spiritual depth of relationship between God and his people by the giving of the Holy Spirit. This comes to expression in the NT teaching that our bodies are now the temples of God (1 Cor. 6:19). But it hardly follows from this new emphasis that God's concern now narrows from the whole of creation to the heart of the individual. Not only is this improbable on theological grounds (as though God loses interest in the larger issues as time goes on), but even a superficial understanding of Jesus' teaching shows that he defined his work entirely within the categories of the OT. He not only assumed but emphasized the continuity of his ministry with the OT promises. If Jesus had meant to introduce another conception of God's concern and program—which would have involved a paradigmatic shift for his hearers, who saw the world in Old Testament categories—he would have had to give it a great deal more emphasis than he did. Of course he had to correct their nationalistic and narrowly political ideas of the kingdom, but he did nothing to indicate that creation and history lay outside the concern of his program. John does quote Jesus as saying that his kingdom was not of this world (John 18:36), but the Greek preposition makes clear that Jesus is saying the kingdom does not have its source in this world order, not that it will not be realized there. We have shown that Jesus' ministry had implications both for creation as a whole and for all the nations. Jesus was broadening the OT promises; one cannot see that he was spiritualizing them.

Interestingly, the very ones that insist on a spiritual

interpretation of Matthew 5:5 or Luke 6:20 are ordinarily those who reject nonliteral interpretations of Scripture. J. Miranda comments on this sort of Bible reading: "I wonder where there is more faith and hope: in believing 'in the God who raises the dead' (Rom. 4:17) or in believing like Luke in the God who 'filled the hungry with good things and sent the rich away empty' (Luke 1:53)?"[4]

The fuller revelation of the NT provides for a deepening and enriching of God's relation with his people and a decisive defeat of sin and death at a fundamental level. But in showing us this great encounter with evil, the NT does not intend us to understand it in isolation from the history of the OT. We saw how emphatically Genesis portrays the progress of sin into every area of culture and into all nations. In portraying Christ as the fulfillment of the promise to Abraham (as Matthew does), we are clearly to understand that the intervention which Genesis 12 pictures has been realized in the ministry of Christ. Though the OT certainly does not ignore the inner reality, the NT deals with the heart in such a way as to convey the fact that the victory of Christ at this depth will issue in nothing less than the resurrection of the whole body and eventually the restoration of all things.

We must recognize also that there is a development in Scripture from more primitive to more complex forms of expression. The NT betrays the influence of Greek philosophy and the consequent ability to symbolize meaning at a higher level of generality. Paul can speak of conscience, John of the *logos*; both can be used to communicate the truth of God's revelation in Christ, and both—scholars point out—maintain essential continuity with OT truth. It would be foolish indeed to ignore the value of such instruments of thought and communication; but it would be equally foolish to feel that now reality has been limited to this higher level of abstraction. These must still be filled out with more concrete forms of expression and the whole range of experience contained in the OT.

The basic reason, of course, for considering matter and

spirit as a whole is that from our discussion of creation we have seen that the spirit cannot be made an object of independent attention, because it does not exist in isolation from its material context. It is in and through the created order that the human person must express his or her values, and it is in this order of things that God wills to be glorified. It is Christianity of all religions of the world that affirms the value of the created order and sees our service in it, however humble, as service to God. This affirmation of the material world has accompanied the gospel witness wherever it has gone. A Western scholar once asked an old Caledonian whether Christianity brought the idea of the soul to the island. "No," replied the old man, "we already knew about that; what Christianity has given us is the notion of the body."[5]

The Individual and the Community
Just as values of the person are mediated in and through the material world, so they must be expressed in terms of their social context. The teaching of Scripture and the study of social sciences both indicate that the structures in which persons live are intrinsic to their humanity. As we can be truly human only in some created context, so we are persons only as a people. Walter Brueggemann expresses the matter in these terms: in Scripture "the unit of decision-making is the community and that always with reference to the land."[6]

To underline this point, we need only remind ourselves that Christ's Lordship has now been extended over all things in heaven and on earth. It follows that no human structure can now lie outside the sphere of his authority or remain indifferent to his purposes. Now all things are challenged by the righteousness that has appeared in his ministry and has been confirmed by his death and resurrection. The cross and the resurrection not only marked the victory over the powers of evil (Col. 2:15), but also represented the invasion of the power of salvation in history, on the earth. It is hard to disagree with Miranda's assertion that "we cannot take seriously the absolute centrality of the resurrection of the body in the NT if the kingdom of justice is not established on earth."[7] The two restorations call for one another.

Sometimes it is felt that the nearness of Christ's return is an excuse for quietism in the social arena. Since Christ is coming soon and things seem to be getting worse (as the NT promised they would!), there appears to be little motivation to exert oneself in this area. But the teaching of the NT is quite the reverse; it is precisely the approach of the end that is a special goad to righteousness (1 Thess. 5:6-11). Norman Gottwald says of the early Christians: "The resolution they foresaw was an impending eruption of an overwhelming and just power that would reconstitute human societies as the single society of the divine warrior through the agency of his triumphant son."[8] So it is precisely the character of this approaching resolution that makes us sensitive to issues of justice in the struggles going on around us.

Leaving social structures to care for themselves while we focus our attention on individuals moreover does nothing to alleviate the problems that we face, and it surely makes our witness more difficult. In fact, it is clear in many areas of life that when our institutions—our media, our educational structures, our political systems—are left to take care of themselves they inevitably become tools of other powers and other value systems. "If economic, political, social and cultural dimensions of human life are not incorporated integrally and holistically into the essence of evangelism and the substance of salvation, they become the playing field of other powers, other gods and idols, other ideologies and world views."[9]

The person then simply cannot be considered in isolation from the structures of his world. He or she will surely reflect them. Now we are often told at this point that when we concentrate on changing the individual through conversion, we will also indirectly have an impact on the society. This of course is true, for people do have influence on the institutions around them. But we must acknowledge the other side of the equation as well: the shape of society influences people and creates an openness or a barrier to the presentation of the gospel and to the realization of God's purposes. We must recognize the "formative influence of fundamental moods and attitudes perpetrated and reinforced by social practices, the mass. media and ethnic and cultural bonds."[10] This is why God is not content to change individuals. Indeed, if he were, why will he one day go to the trouble of creating a wholly new environment in which the righteousness of his people may shine? Our mission, then, must relate to these realities if it is to reflect the whole of God's purposes. And this means that our mission will include an increasingly sophisticated analysis of our sociopolitical situation in order to inform our obedience.

All of this extends and affirms the integrity of creation and its importance in the program of God. In some traditions creation is a mask, something to be gotten out of the way in order to get to God. The biblical view by contrast is one in which creation is a fit and necessary vehicle for the glory of God. While only the new creation will fully reflect this glory, because of the firstfruits of the Holy Spirit that new order may be already glimpsed. Obviously no present political or social system can be final, but as Wolfhart Pannenberg reminds us, the future kingdom of God demands a particular obedience already in the present and has released a dynamic to direct that obedience. "The satisfaction is not in the perfection of that with which we begin but in the glory of that toward which we tend."[11]

Doing and Telling

The essential message of Scripture is that the Creator God has intervened in this world to make it and its history conform to his purposes. The climax of this work is the death, resurrection and exaltation of Jesus. By these events mankind has been called to a new responsibility before God. The missionary call is that which gives each person opportunity to choose freedom by becoming a child of God, a brother or sister to others and a lord of nature.[12] The central question is whether a person will choose this freedom or be bound by nature (or the new nature, technology).

This means that the world is marked by a new potential; "no corner of the world is now left to the sovereignty of human autonomy."[13] As all men are called to respond to this new situation, all cultures have a new obligation to God; and every corner of reality reverberates with this spiritual struggle.

Signs of the presence of the kingdom are visible to the one who has faith (though not perhaps on the front page of the newspaper). "Visibility does not always mean recognition, and it never means recognition without faith."[14] The value system of a fallen world overlooks the spread of the Church and the one who feeds the hungry. Remember the story of the poor wise man—though everyone forgot him, he really had saved the city (Eccles. 9:13-18).

On the other hand, according to Scripture even the darkness is a sign of Christ's reign. The suffering of God's people is the "unavoidable and recognizable indication of the presence of this kingdom on earth."[15] This is why the NT insists on speaking of it in the same breath with joy (Jas. 1:2). Apostasy too, as we saw, is a sign of the truth and a necessary condition for the appearance of the Antichrist (1 Tim. 4:1). And in the end natural and supernatural disasters are sent by God to shock a jaded world into repenting and believing the gospel. This darkness is all a part of Christ's reign and not a peculiar exception to it.

Now let us ask what implication this has for our telling or showing the gospel. It is obvious, first of all, that the proclamation of the gospel must have a central place in our witness. From the beginning of the Church there was the understanding that "one must have heard of Christ in order to be able to believe on him. Thus he must be preached everywhere."[16] Something has happened in history to which men and women must respond. Preaching the gospel calls them to account. Everything, however, depends on the nature of the message. Unfortunately our discussions of evangelism seem fixated on methods and often assume the message. Evangelism in the Bible was never a matter of transferring some ideas from one mind to another. However simple the message may have been, it was always the encounter of one view of the world with another. God is Creator, and Christ has come to mediate the salvation both of mankind and the whole created order; the Holy Spirit is the sign of this victory and an anticipation of its consummation. This imperial perspective must challenge every other world-view.

So when we speak of the gospel we are speaking of a mighty remaking and an earth-shaking binding of Satan. We are not pointing to words, but our words are pointing to a reality which has gripped us and the world and which therefore must have some point of reference in our lives and families. The early Church couldn't stop talking about what had happened, but neither could they avoid demonstrating the power that had grasped them—displaying an unheard of unity between Jew and Greek, a special care for widows and orphans, and above all a keen anticipation of God's promised renewal of all things.

Our words then have become a part of God's mighty redemptive program, our telling a part of his doing. In this light one can understand Mennonite C. Norman Kraus's insistence that "communication of the gospel includes both saying and doing, but doing must be used as the more comprehensive category."[17] As in John's portrayal of Jesus, words are also acts, pointers.

Our words are essential, but only because we speak the truth. And the truth is that the powers of the new age are present: forgiveness, the Holy Spirit and righteousness. Because of the character of this present period, by our actual lived response to the gospel we either become part of the making of the kingdom or part of its opposition.[18] There must be a congruence between the message and the act of communicating; "the end to which the evangelist points, the fulfillment of the vision of shalom, should appear in the act of pointing."[19] The reason again lies in the nature of proclamation as an encounter between one reality (God's power) and all other conceptions of power.

It is commonly recognized in communication theory

that if the behavior of the messenger and the environment in which the process takes place do not support what is being said, the message will not be heard. So telling, even though central, does not and cannot exist by itself. It always takes place in a context that will either support or impede what is being said. Karl Barth concludes: "What is vital is that the evangelizing community should say what it has to say to those around in a glad and spirited and peaceful way corresponding to its content."[20]

Perhaps we need to give some thought to the category of redemptive action. That is, we should seek to shape our vocations and our communities in such a way that they become images of the restorative character of the law and of God's remaking work displayed in Christ. That is, we will not only use our vocation as a platform to speak of Christ (though we should not neglect this), but we will also seek to make our work an incarnation of the values of the kingdom, which can in turn become a commentary on our witness. We say to people, "You see, this is what I mean by the gospel." In this sense healing and social work become "an expression of the redemptive action of God made manifest to the world order in and through the redeemed community."[21]

Faith and Works

Our study has made clear the priority of faith as the response to what God does for our salvation. God delivered us in Christ while we were helpless to save ourselves, and our life with God begins by recognizing this. But matters do not end there. For the moment of our receiving God's grace is artificial when it is abstracted from the whole movement of God to us and of the person to God. When faith reaches out to receive, the Holy Spirit energizes and converts. It is in the heart where the gospel penetrates and does its initial work, but that is just the beginning. The seed planted in our hearts is meant to grow in our lives and bloom in our communities. The Christian faith does not reside in a particular sphere of our life, but becomes an aspect of the whole of life.

Response and action then are not only allowed in the

missionary call, but are inevitable. Just as it is artificial to make a separation between the response of faith and that of obedience, so it is impossible to isolate our mission of verbal witness from that of loving identification. The one may address the heart and mind, the other may be more visible and concrete, but in the end they call for one another.

Jesus suggests that his own ministry is the model for ours. As the Father sent him, so he sends us. So his presence among us as a houseboy (Luke 22:27) should be a primary model for the character of Christian mission. When brought face-to-face with the situation of poverty and oppression, can we remain indifferent? Is not a part of our witness the character of the response we make? Missiologist Jerry Gort notes, "At root, conditions of poverty, suffering and want are situations of injustice and ipso facto, are the work of human hands and therefore a matter of ethical judgment."[22] The truth is that skepticism and neutrality in these issues are only possible for those uninvolved in their reality. Robert Gordis comments: "Skepticism is a state of mind possible only for those who observe and dislike evil, but are not its direct victims. Those who are direct sufferers are impelled either to change the conditions or to seek to escape from them."[23] Such neutrality therefore is obviously impossible for those who model their ministry after the Lord, who came precisely to share in the suffering of his people and to articulate their cry to the Lord. Perhaps then it is only in our working with those in need that we will be able to help them articulate their first cry of help to God.

We may conclude this portion by recalling the image of dramatic movement with which we began our study. The work of God has called us on the stage. We have lines to speak that are essential to the dramatic character of history, but they only make sense in the movement of the whole. And this movement, the NT says, features a lifestyle of loving hospitality which matches our verbal invitation to join God's own fellowship.

Mission and Development

After this lengthy detour we are ready to answer our initial questions about the relation between the mission God sends his people to accomplish and the work of making the world a better and more human place in which to live. Our conclusion may be given in two related theses.

1. The meaning of these last days is mission. We have concluded that the central fact of this period of time is that God has granted the world one last period of grace, one little time in which people may come to him. And this meaning is made plain primarily in the proclamation of the gospel. So, as J. Blauw puts it, "the proclamation of the gospel is the form of the kingdom of God."[24] Moreover, it belongs to the nature of the Church to announce and proclaim this message (1 Pet. 2:9, 10). The message that the Church speaks of, however, encompasses the whole of God's purposes for creation in its purview. All these purposes have now come to focus on Christ whom God has determined will have the preeminence in all things. At this point we must be very careful not to divide up what God has brought together. John Stott, for example, insists that "God the creator is constantly active in the world in providence, in common grace and judgment, quite apart from the purposes for which he sent his Son, his Spirit and his Church into the world."[25] But our study has shown us that these more comprehensive actions of God are now focused on the redemptive purposes revealed in Christ and announced in the Church. For it is through this means that God has now purposed to glorify himself. It is our theological categories and not the teaching of Scripture that have made God's general providence possess purposes "quite apart" from his special grace. It is the treasure of the gospel that now gives to this period its unique character and to the world its special opportunity to hear God's word or reject it, to be hopeful or resigned.

2. The meaning of development is mission. It follows from this that the ultimate meaning of any genuine development lies in the purposes God has for this world. The yearning of people around us is really a desire to enjoy the fruits of the kingdom of God. We Christians therefore should feel as deeply as possible the reality of these longings. Augustine of Hippo understood this and expressed it in his sermons:

I know you want to keep on living. You do not want to die. And you want to pass from this life to another in such a way that you will not rise again as a dead man, but fully alive and transformed. This is what you desire. . . . I have no patience with that spurious "strength of character" that puts up patiently with the absence of good things. Do we not all long for the future Jerusalem? . . . I cannot refrain from this longing; I would be inhuman if I could.[26]

People around us suffering from various burdens may know nothing of the gospel, but "for the stuff of that kingdom (they) yearn; even thousands who have never in their lives darkened a church door grope blindly after it unwittingly. For the hope of it is engraved in the very necessity of man's nature, and he can no more escape it than he can escape himself."[27]

So these hopes do not lie outside the scope of the gospel. But how do they relate to the hope that centers in Jesus Christ? There are at least two ways that this relationship may be explained. First, all genuine development is a reflection and fruit of the gospel. It is no accident that social and medical work has accompanied the gospel from the beginning. Wherever the gospel has gone, it has encouraged elements vital to growth and progress: a sense of the dignity of the person, the ability to set and work toward goals, the sense of responsibility toward creation and each other, and that most important of all ingredients in any program of development—hope that things can change, that the world can be different than it is. Whatever names these values go under, and whatever their immediate source, there can be no question that they belong to Christ and reflect his purposes for the world. As mediator of creation and Lord of the new creation he claims every pursuit of goodness and truth for his kingdom. Even where historically such attitudes have no connection with the Church, we insist they are reflected light of the gospel. And we insist furthermore that many who serve such ideals perform a distant service to Christ's kingdom without knowing it. But it is not hard to show that more often than not these fruits not only theologically but historically are fruit from the tree of the gospel. "Wherever the missionary endeavor has gone, the curious situation arises that a whole nation gratefully eats the fruit, but only a minority desire the tree which produces the fruit."[28]

These, then, are indirect signs of Christ's Lordship, and we ought not to be ungrateful even for this distant light. Of course this is not enough; a reflected light does not provide illumination for what the NT calls the works of day. Therefore we must describe a second way in which development relates to mission. However good the work of development may be, only the gospel can properly interpret this work and give it its meaning. That is, only the Christian witness can point people to the light that is reflected in the work of development and provide it with a larger framework in which its full meaning may be seen. Yes, people need to have the opportunity to realize their gifts and abilities, but that is because they are created in God's image and may now be remade in Christ's. Yes, justice must be done in our community, but this is because Christ's Lordship is to be reflected in all human authorities. Orlando Costas explains further this function: "the Church is faithful to her mission not only by showing forth her commitment to justice and peace but also by interpreting the meaning of the struggles of men for a better world in the light of the gospel."[29] As Christ is the content of God's promises, so he is the object of people's search. This means that this "is not a world without hope, just as on the same ground it cannot be simply a lost world or a completely loveless and unsanctified world . . . it will find the essence of all creaturely glory in serving him, actively siding with him and in this way . . . being clothed with all the honor and also with all the joy and peace of eternal life."[30]

As long as we understand the fullness of God's purposes, there is no need to change our language. We may still call missionaries those who are called to cross cultural boundaries to proclaim the gospel, and evangelists those who are gifted to announce the message of salvation. There will still be missions—that is, the sending of people to plant churches in another cultural setting. But God's mission is too large and important to be left to missionaries! For God desires that all the gifts of the Church be employed in the great work of making his glory known among the nations. Such a broadening of our Christian responsibility should not frustrate us; it is not our work after all, it is God's. But it may give us a more healthy respect for the diversity of gifts within the body of Christ. Meanwhile, the limitation of time and resources will not force us to narrow our focus, but it will teach us a stewardship in which—reflecting God's own economy of means—nothing is wasted and no one is overlooked. For in the end it is not a matter of resources but of vision. And we of all people who live in the shadow of God's breathtaking redemption ought to have the hope that keeps us faithful to the whole of God's promised future.

Notes

Introduction

1. Gustavo Gutierrez, *A Theology of Liberation* (Maryknoll, N.Y.: Orbis, 1973), pp. 36, 37.
2. in *Your Kingdom Come* (Geneva: World Council of Churches; New York: Friendship Press, 1980), p. 229.
3. Peter Beyerhaus, *Theological Foundations for Mission* (Grand Rapids, Mich.: Zondervan, 1972), p. 52.
4. *Ibid.*, p. 62.
5. Arthur Johnston, *The Battle for World Evangelism* (Wheaton, Ill.: Tyndale House, 1978), p. 18.
6. See Orlando E. Costas, *The Church and Its Mission: A Shattering Critique from the Third World* (Wheaton, Ill.: Tyndale House, 1974); Waldron Scott, *Bring Forth Justice: A Contemporary Perspective on Mission* (Grand Rapids, Mich.: Eerdmans, 1980); John R. W. Stott, *Christian Mission in the Modern World* (Downers Grove, Ill.: InterVarsity Press, 1975).
7. (Downers Grove, Ill.: InterVarsity Press, 1977).
8. See, for example, Robert Lincoln Hancock, editor, *The Ministry of Development in Evangelical Perspective* (Pasadena, Calif.: William Carey Library, 1979) or Ronald J. Sider, editor, *Evangelicals and Development* (London: Marshall Morgan & Scott, 1981).
9. See Walter Eichrodt, *Man in the Old Testament*, K. and R. Smith, trans., Studies in Biblical Theology 4 (London: SCM, 1951), p. 8.
10. See Bernard S. Childs, *Biblical Theology in Crisis* (Philadelphia: Westminster, 1970).
11. Bernard S. Childs, *Introduction to the Old Testament as Scripture* (Philadelphia: Fortress, 1979), p. 76.
12. David Baker, *Two Testaments: One Bible* (Downers Grove, Ill.: InterVarsity Press, 1977), p. 267.
13. in *op. cit.*, Costas, *The Church and Its Mission*, p. 284.
14. See Erich Auerbach, *Mimesis: The Representation of Reality in Western Literature* (Princeton, N.J.: Princeton University Press, 1953).
15. J. R. R. Tolkien, "On Fairy Stories," in C. S. Lewis, editor, *Essays Presented to Charles Williams* (New York: Oxford University Press, 1947), pp. 83, 84.

16. Jose Miguez-Bonino, *Doing Theology in a Revolutionary Situation* (Philadelphia: Fortress, 1975), p. 138.

1. Creation of the World

1. Gerhard von Rad, *Genesis*, John Mark, trans. (Philadelphia: Westminster, 1961), pp. 34, 35.
2. Herman Gunkel, *The Legends of Genesis: The Biblical Saga and History* (New York: Schocken Books, 1964), p. 65.
3. See W. A. Dyrness, "Old Testament Aesthetics," Ward and Laural Gasque, editors, H. R. Rookmaaker memorial volume, forthcoming.
4. Claus Westermann, *Creation*, John J. Scullion, trans. (London: Society for the Propagation of Christian Knowledge, 1974), p. 61.
5. *Ibid.*, p. 63.
6. *Ibid.*, p. 46.
7. See Colin Brown, editor, *The New International Dictionary of New Testament Theology*, Vol. I (Grand Rapids, Mich.: Zondervan, 1976-78), p. 208.
8. Walter Kaiser, *Toward an Old Testament Theology* (Grand Rapids, Mich.: Zondervan, 1978), p. 76.
9. *Op. cit.*, Westermann, *Creation*, p. 46.

2. The Creation of Man and Woman

1. Karl Barth, *Church Dogmatics*, III/1 (Edinburgh: T & T Clark, 1936), p. 192.
2. H. W. Wolff, *Anthropology of the Old Testament*, M. Kohl, trans. (Philadelphia: Fortress, 1974), p. 24.
3. *Op. cit.*, Eichrodt, *Man in the Old Testament*, p. 33.
4. St. Augustine, *Confessions*, IV, The Harvard Classics, Charles W. Eliot, editor (New York: P. F. Collier & Son, 1937), p. 53.
5. C. Norman Kraus, *The Healing Christ* (Scottdale, Pa.: Herald Press, 1972), p. 34.
6. *Op. cit.*, Eichrodt, *Man in the Old Testament*, p. 9.
7. *Op. cit.*, Westermann, *Creation*, p. 60.
8. in Richard J. Mouw, *Politics and the Biblical Drama* (Grand Rapids, Mich.: Eerdmans, 1976), p. 27.
9. See Walter Brueggemann, *The Land* (Philadelphia: Fortress, 1977), p. 105n.
10. *Op. cit.*, Barth, *Church Dogmatics*, IV/1, p. 113.
11. *Op. cit.*, Westermann, *Creation*, p. 51.
12. See R. David Freedman, "Woman, a Power Equal to Man," *Biblical Archaeology Review*, January-February 1983, pp. 56-58.
13. *Op. cit.* Barth, *Church Dogmatics*, IV/1, p. 113.

3. The Fall and Expulsion from the Garden

1. Claus Westermann, *A Thousand Years and a Day* (Philadelphia: Muhlenberg, 1962), p. 11.
2. See *op. cit.*, Kaiser, *Toward an Old Testament Theology*, p. 77.
3. John Milton, *Paradise Lost* (New York: New American Library, 1961), pp. 254, 255.
4. See *op. cit.*, Kaiser, *Toward an Old Testament Theology*, p. 80.
5. See *op. cit.*, Westermann, *Creation*, p. 22.
6. See *op cit.*, Eichrodt, *Man in the Old Testament*, p. 36.

4. The Call of Abraham

1. *Op. cit.*, Brueggemann, *The Land*, p. 16.
2. See *op. cit.*, Gunkel, *The Legends of Genesis*, p. 79.
3. See James Muilenburg, "Abraham and the Nations," *Interpretation* 19 (1965):397.
4. See William F. Albright, "From the Patriarchs to Moses," *The Biblical Archaeologist* 36 (1973):7-15.
5. *Ibid.*
6. See David J. A. Clines, *The Theme of the Pentateuch* (Sheffield: University of Sheffield, 1978), pp. 32-43.
7. See *op. cit.*, von Rad, *Genesis*, p. 43.
8. See *op. cit.*, Clines, *The Theme of the Pentateuch*, p. 29.
9. See *ibid.*, p. 77.
10. See Lesslie Newbigin, *The Open Secret* (Grand Rapids, Mich.: Eerdmans, 1978), p. 76.
11. Claus Westermann, "God and His People: The Church in the Old Testament," *Interpretation* 17 (1963):260.

5. The Rescue of God's People

1. See Claus Westermann, "The Role of Lament in the Theology of the Old Testament," *Interpretation* 28 (1974):20-38.
2. See *op. cit.*, Albright, "From the Patriarchs to Moses," p. 55.
3. See H. H. Rowley, *The Missionary Message of the Old Testament* (London: Carey Press, 1944), pp. 14, 15.
4. See William Dyrness, *Themes in Old Testament Theology*, (Downers Grove, Ill.: InterVarsity Press, 1979), pp. 30-32.
5. On all this see E. F. Campbell, Jr., "Moses and the Foundation of Israel," *Interpretation* 29 (1975):145, 146.
6 See Gerhard von Rad, *Old Testament Theology*, Vol. II, D. M. G. Stalker, trans. (New York: Harper & Row, 1965), p. 164.
7. *Op. cit.*, Westermann, "God and His People," p. 263.
8. *Op. cit.*, Gutierrez, *A Theology of Liberation*, p. 159.
9. See Walter Brueggemann, *Living Towards a Vision: Biblical Reflections on Shalom* (Philadelphia: United Church Press, 1976), p. 56.
10. *Op. cit.*, Campbell, "Moses and the Foundation of Israel."
11. *Op. cit.*, Brueggemann, *Living Towards a Vision*, p. 64.
12. in J. D. Douglas, editor, *New Bible Dictionary* (Grand Rapids, Mich.: Eerdmans, 1975), p. 723.
13. Herbert B. Huffmon, "The Treaty Background of the Hebrew YADA," *Bulletin of American School of Oriental Research* 181/184 (1966):31, 33.
14. Jose Miranda, *Marx and the Bible: A Critique of the Philosophy of Oppression* (Maryknoll, N.Y.: Orbis, 1974), p. 93.
15. See *op. cit.*, Eichrodt, *Man in the Old Testament*, pp. 11, 12.
16. *Ibid.*, pp. 16, 17.
17. H. W. Wolff, "Masters and Slaves," *Interpretation* 27 (1973):269.
18. J. van Selms, in *Interpreter's Dictionary of the Bible. Supplementary Volume*, Keith R. Crim *et al*, editors (Nashville: Abingdon, 1976), p. 498.

6. Entrance into Canaan

1. Patrick D. Miller, Jr., "The Blessing of God," *Interpretation* 29 (1975):244

2. *Ibid.*, p. 248.
3. See *op. cit.*, Brueggemann, *The Land*, p. 31.
4. Walter Harrelson, "Guidance in the Wilderness," *Interpretation* 13 (1959):28.
5. See *op. cit.*, von Rad, *Old Testament Theology*, Vol. I (New York: Harper & Row, 1962), p. 282.
6. *Op. cit.*, von Rad, *Genesis*.
7. *Ibid.*, p. 10.
8. See Patrick D. Miller, Jr., "The Gift of God: The Deuteronomic Theology of the Land," *Interpretation* 23 (1969):459.
9. James A. Sanders, "Torah and Christ," *Interpretation* 29 (1975):381.
10. *Op. cit.*, Miller, "The Gift of God," p. 455.
11. L. E. Toombs, in *op. cit.*, *Interpreter's Dictionary of the Bible*, IV, p. 797.
12. John Wenham, *The Goodness of God* (Downers Grove, Ill.: InterVarsity Press, 1974), p. 125.
13. *Op. cit.*, Brueggemann, *The Land*, p. 94.
14. James A. Wharton, "The Secret of Y," *Interpretation* 27 (1973):58.
15. Georg Fohrer, in *Theological Dictionary of the New Testament*, Vol. VII, Gerhard Kittel and Gerhard Friedrich, editors (Grand Rapids, Mich.: Eerdmans, 1970), p. 973.

7. The Monarchy

1. See *op. cit.*, Wolff, "Masters and Slaves," p. 260.
2. See Dennis J. McCarthy, "The Inauguration of Monarchy in Israel: A Form Critical Study of 1 Samuel 8—12," *Interpretation* 27 (1973):401-412.
3. *Ibid.*, p. 412.
4. See John Bright, *Covenant and Promise: The Prophetic Understanding of the Future in Pre-Exilic Israel* (Philadelphia: Westminster, 1976), pp. 111-123.
5. Dennis J. McCarthy, "II Samuel and the Structure of Deuteronomic History," *Journal of Biblical Literature* 84 (1965):136.
6. *Op. cit.*, Bright, *Covenant and Promise*, p. 66.
7. Shemaryahu Talmon, "The Biblical Concept of Jerusalem," *Journal of Ecumenical Studies* 8 (1974):309.
8. See *op. cit.*, Wolff, "Masters and Slaves," pp. 259-272; George Mendenhall, "The Monarchy," *Interpretation* 29 (1975):155-170; Walter Brueggemann, "David and His Theologian," *Catholic Biblical Quarterly* 30 (1968):156-181, and *op. cit.*, *The Land*, pp. 82-89.
9. *Op. cit.*, Mendenhall, "The Monarchy," p. 155.
10. *Ibid.*, p. 166.
11. *Op. cit.*, Brueggemann, *The Land*, p. 86.
12. See *op. cit.*, Mendenhall, "The Monarchy," p. 170.
13. *Op. cit.*, Wolff, "Masters and Slaves," p. 261.
14. See *op. cit.*, Mendenhall, "The Monarchy," p. 157.
15. See *op. cit.*, Westermann, "God and His People," pp. 267, 268.
16. See *op. cit.*, Brueggemann, "David and His Theologian," pp. 156-181.
17. *Op. cit.*, Eichrodt, *Man in the Old Testament*, p. 19.
18. See David M. Gunn, "David and the Gift of the Kingdom," *Semeia* (Society of Biblical Literature) 3 (1975):14-45.
19. See *op. cit.*, Rowley, *The Missionary Message of the Old Testament*, p. 32.
20. See Robert Gordis, *Poets, Prophets and Sages: Essays in Biblical Interpretation* (Bloomington, Ind.: Indiana University Press, 1971), p. 162.

21. Derek Kidner, *Proverbs* (London: Tyndale, 1964), p. 79.

8. The Prophets

1. Walter Brueggemann, *The Prophetic Imagination* (Philadelphia: Fortress, 1978), p. 32.
2. See *op. cit.*, Eichrodt, *Man in the Old Testament*, pp. 20-22.
3. Bernard S. Childs, "The Canonical Shape of the Prophetic Literature," *Interpretation* 32 (1978):49.
4. *Ibid.*, p. 50.
5. Walter Eichrodt, "The Holy One in Your Midst: The Theology of Hosea," *Interpretation* 15 (1961):259.
6. *Ibid.*, p. 269.

9. Eviction from the Land

1. See *op. cit.*, Eichrodt, *Man in the Old Testament*, pp. 20-22.
2. See Hendrikus Berkhof, *Christ the Meaning of History*, L. Buurman, trans. (London: SCM, 1966), p. 53.
3. *Op. cit.*, Brueggemann, *The Prophetic Imagination*, p. 51.
4. See *op. cit.*, Bright, *Covenant and Promise*, p. 165.
5. *Op. cit.*, Brueggemann, *The Land*, p. 111. See also *op. cit.*, Bright, *Covenant and Promise*, p. 185.
6. *Op. cit.*, Sanders, "Torah and Christ," p. 383.
7. W. D. Davies, *The Gospel and the Land: Early Christianity and Jewish Territorial Doctrine* (Berkeley, Calif.: University of California Press, 1974), p. 39.
8. See Sheldon Blank, "Prophet as Paradigm," in *Essays in Old Testament Ethics*, J. L. Crenshaw and J. T. Willis, editors (New York: KTAV, 1974), pp. 111-130.
9. *Ibid.*, p. 126.
10. See *op. cit.*, Kaiser, *Toward an Old Testament Theology*, p. 233.
11. *Op. cit.*, Bright, *Covenant and Promise*, p. 194.
12. Walter Zimmerli, "The Message of the Prophet Ezekiel," *Interpretation* 23 (1969):148.
13. *Op. cit.*, Bright, *Covenant and and Promise*, p. 189.
14. *Op. cit.*, Brueggemann, *The Prophetic Imagination*, p. 75.
15. *Op. cit.*, Mouw, *Politics and the Biblical Drama*, p. 106.
16. See Joachim Jeremias, *Jesus' Promise to the Nations*, Studies in Biblical Theology 24 (London: SCM, 1967), pp. 58-65.
17. David Noel Freedman, " 'Son of Man, Can These Bones Live?' The Exile," *Interpretation* 29 (1975):185.
18. See *op. cit.*, Kaiser, *Toward an Old Testament Theology*, p. 212.
19. Ferdinand Hahn, *Mission in the New Testament*, Frank Clarke, trans., Studies in Biblical Theology 47 (Naperville, Ill.: Allenson, 1965), p. 19.
20. in *op. cit.*, *Interpreter's Dictionary of the Bible*, II, p. 405.
21. *Op. cit.*, Rowley, *The Missionary Message of the Old Testament*, p. 58.
22. *Op. cit.*, Wolff, "Masters and Slaves," p. 266.
23. See *op. cit.*, Rowley, *The Missionary Message of the Old Testament*, p. 54.
24. See *op. cit.*, Freedman, " 'Son of Man, Can These Bones Live?' ", p. 186.
25. *Op. cit.*, Berkhof, *Christ the Meaning of History*, p. 51.
26. *Ibid.*, p. 53.
27. *Op. cit.*, Childs, *Introduction to the Old Testament as Scripture*, p. 622.

28. Johannes Blauw, *The Missionary Nature of the Church: A Survey of the Biblical Theology of Mission* (Grand Rapids, Mich.: Eerdmans, 1962), p. 82.

10. Between the Testaments: A Distant Hope
1. See *op. cit.*, Rowley, *The Missionary Message of the Old Testament*, p. 65.
2. See *op. cit.*, Jeremias, *Jesus' Promise to the Nations*, pp. 11-16.
3. See Martin Hengel, *Judaism and Hellenism* (Philadelphia: Fortress, 1974).
4. See Paul D. Hanson, "Old Testament Apocalyptic Reconsidered," *Interpretation* 25 (1971):468.
5. *Ibid.*, p. 479.
6. G. E. Ladd, "Apocalyptic and New Testament Theology," in *Reconciliation and Hope*, R. Banks, editor (Grand Rapids, Mich.: Eerdmans, 1974), pp. 291, 292.
7. See Eduard Lohse, *The New Testament Environment*, J. S. Steely, trans. (Nashville: Abingdon, 1976), pp. 80, 81.
8. See John 3:16; and *op. cit.*, *Interpreter's Dictionary of the Bible, Supplementary Volume*, p. 663.
9. See *op. cit.*, Lohse, *The New Testament Environment*, p. 76.
10. Günter Klein, "The Biblical Understanding of the Kingdom of God," *Interpretation* 26 (1970):399.
11. See Joseph Bonsirven, *Palestinian Judaism in the Time of Christ*, William Wolf, trans. (New York: Holt, Rinehart and Winston, 1964), pp. 172-174.
12. *Ibid.*
13. R. N. Longenecker, *Paul the Apostle of Liberty* (Grand Rapids, Mich.: Baker, 1976), p. 84.

11. Jesus Christ: The Coming of the Kingdom
1. Martin Hengel, *Property and Riches in the Early Church* (Philadelphia: Fortress, 1974), p. 15.
2. Wolfhart Pannenberg, in *Theology and the Kingdom of God*, R. J. Neuhaus, editor (Philadelphia: Westminster, 1969), p. 55.
3. See I. H. Marshall, *The Gospel of Luke* (Grand Rapids, Mich.: Eerdmans, 1978), p. 184.
4. See *op. cit.*, Jeremias, *Jesus' Promise to the Nations*, p. 45.
5. *Op. cit.*, Marshall, *The Gospel of Luke*, p. 476.
6. W. G. Kümmel, *Theology of the New Testament*, J. D. Steely, trans. (London: SCM, 1974), p. 36.
7. C. H. Dodd, *The Founder of Christianity* (London: Macmillan, 1970), p. 55.
8. Joachim Jeremias, *The Parables of Jesus*, S. H. Hooke, trans. (London: SCM, 1972), p. 149.
9. See Herman Ridderbos, *The Coming of the Kingdom* (Philadelphia: Presbyterian and Reformed, 1962), pp. 147, 148.
10. *Op. cit.*, Jeremias, *The Parables of Jesus*, p. 230.
11. Geerhardus Vos, *Pauline Eschatology* (Grand Rapids, Mich.: Eerdmans, 1952), p. 38.
12. See *op. cit.*, Ladd, "Apocalyptic and New Testament Theology," pp. 293, 294.
13. Joachim Jeremias, *New Testament Theology*, John Bowden, trans. (New York: Scribner's, 1971), p. 112.
14. See *op. cit.*, Ridderbos, *The Coming of the Kingdom*, pp. 189, 190.
15. *Ibid.*

16. *Op. cit.*, Sanders, "Torah and Christ," p. 384.
17. *Op. cit.*, Jeremias, *New Testament Theology*, pp. 63-68.
18. See *op. cit.*, Sanders, "Torah and Christ" and G. E. Ladd, *Jesus and the Kingdom* (New York: Harper & Row, 1964), p. 110.
19. *Op. cit.*, Ridderbos, *The Coming of the Kingdom*, p. 65.
20. *Op. cit.*, Dodd, *The Founder of Christianity*, p. 41.
21. See *op. cit.*, Jeremias, *Jesus' Promise to the Nations*, pp. 62, 63.
22. Paul Minear, *And Great Shall Be Your Reward* (New Haven, Conn.: Yale University Press, 1942), p. 43.
23. Karl Barth, "An Exegetical Study of Matthew 28:16-20," in *Theology of Christian Mission*, Gerald Anderson, editor (New York: Abingdon, 1961), p. 62.
24. *Op. cit.*, Costas, *The Church and Its Mission*, p. 243.
25. Vincent Taylor, *The Gospel According to St. Mark* (London: Macmillan, 1966), p. 423.
26. *Op. cit.*, Dodd, *The Founder of Christianity*, p. 62.
27. See *op. cit.*, *New International Dictionary of New Testament Theology*, I, p. 358.
28. *Op. cit.*, Dodd, *The Founder of Christianity*, p. 64.
29. John Howard Yoder, *The Politics of Jesus* (Grand Rapids, Mich.: Eerdmans, 1972), esp. p. 175.
30. *Op. cit.*, Mouw, *Politics and the Biblical Drama*.
31. *Op. cit.*, Ridderbos, *The Coming of the Kingdom*, pp. 143, 144.

12. The Death and Resurrection of Christ

1. John R. Donahue, "Jesus as the Parable of God in the Gospel of Mark," *Interpretation* 32 (1978):370.
2. Paul J. Achtemeier, "Mark as Interpreter of the Jesus Tradition," *Interpretation* 32 (1978):339-352.
3. *Ibid.*, p. 342.
4. *Op. cit.*, Jeremias, *New Testament Theology*, pp. 69, 70.
5. *Op. cit.*, Hahn, *Mission in the New Testament*, p. 112.
6. *Ibid.*, p. 40.
7. *Op. cit.*, Donahue, "Jesus as the Parable of God," pp. 378, 379.
8. *Op. cit.*, Wenham, *The Goodness of God*, p. 170.
9. See Oscar Cullmann, *Christ and Time*, F. Filson, trans. (Philadelphia: Westminster, 1946).
10. See Jack Dean Kingsbury, "The Structure of Matthew's Gospel and His Concept of Salvation-History," *Catholic Biblical Quarterly* 35 (1973):451-474.
11. See Gerhard Barth, "Matthew's Understanding of the Law," in G. Bornkamm, Gerhard Barth and H. J. Held, *Tradition and Interpretation in Matthew*, Percy Scott, trans. (Philadelphia: Westminster, 1963), pp. 109-121.
12. See *op. cit.*, Jeremias, *Jesus' Promise to the Nations*, pp. 55-58.
13. See *op. cit.*, W. D. Davies, *The Gospel and the Land*, p. 249.
14. *Op. cit.*, Hahn, *Mission in the New Testament*, p. 212.
15. *Ibid.*, p. 127.
16. *Op. cit.*, G. Barth, "Matthew's Understanding of the Law," p. 134.
17. *Op. cit.*, K. Barth, "An Exegetical Study of Matthew 28:16-20," p. 62.
18. *Op. cit.*, Ridderbos, *The Coming of the Kingdom*, p. 252.

19. *Ibid.*, p. 375.
20. *Ibid.*, p. 376.
21. *Op. cit.*, Barth, "An Exegetical Study of Matthew 28:16-20," p. 64.
22. *Op. cit.*, Ridderbos, *The Coming of the Kingdom*, p. 387.
23. See *op. cit.*, G. Barth, "Matthew's Understanding of the Law," pp. 135-137.
24. W. C. Robinson, in *op. cit.*, *Interpreter's Dictionary of the Bible, Supplementary Volume*, p. 560.
25. Paul Minear, *To Heal and to Reveal: Prophetic Vocation According to Luke* (New York: Seabury, 1976), pp. 31, 32.
26. *Ibid.*, p. 64.
27. *Op. cit.*, Jeremias, *Jesus' Promise to the Nations*, p. 63.
28. See Luke 5:32 and *op. cit.*, Hahn, *Mission in the New Testament*, p. 131.

13. The Early Church in Mission

1. See Gabriel Fackre, *Word in Deed: Theological Themes in Evangelism* (Grand Rapids, Mich.: Eerdmans, 1975), pp. 75-77.
2. See C. H. Dodd, *The Apostolic Preaching and Its Developments* (London: Hodder & Stoughton, 1944), p. 33.
3. *Op. cit.*, Ridderbos, *The Coming of the Kingdom*, pp. 258, 259.
4. See *op. cit.*, Minear, *To Heal and to Reveal*, p. 136.
5. John Calvin, *Institutes of the Christian Religion*, II (Philadelphia: Westminster, 1960), pp. xvi, 14.
6. *Op. cit.*, Hahn, *Mission in the New Testament*, p. 50.
7. See *op. cit.*, Dodd, *The Apostolic Preaching*, pp. 21-23.
8. See I. H. Marshall, *Luke: Historian and Theologian* (Grand Rapids, Mich.: Zondervan, 1971), p. 169.
9. *Ibid.*, p. 200.
10. *Op. cit.*, Hahn, *Mission in the New Testament*, p. 134.
11. *Op. cit.*, Dodd, *The Apostolic Preaching*, p. 17.
12. Herman Ridderbos, *Paul: An Outline of His Theology*, J. R. DeWitt, trans. (Grand Rapids, Mich.: Eerdmans, 1975), p. 48.
13. A. N. Wilder, "Kerygma, Eschatology and Social Ethics," in *The Background of the New Testament and Its Eschatology*, W. D. Davies and D. Daube, editors (New York: Cambridge University Press, 1964), p. 519.
14. *Op. cit.*, Brueggemann, *The Land*, p. 178.
15. See *op. cit.*, Wilder, "Kerygma, Eschatology and Social Ethics," pp. 527-530.
16. See *op. cit.*, Fackre, *Word in Deed*, p. 85.
17. *Op. cit.*, Wilder, "Kerygma, Eschatology and Social Ethics," p. 529.
18. See Keith F. Nickle, *The Collection: A Study in Paul's Strategy*, Studies in Biblical Theology 48 (London: SCM, 1966), pp. 100-130.
19. in *op. cit.*, Blauw, *The Missionary Nature of the Church*, p. 117.
20. Oscar Cullmann, "Eschatology and Missions in the New Testament," in *op. cit.*, *The Background of the New Testament and Its Eschatology*, p. 418.
21. *Op. cit.*, Berkhof, *Christ the Meaning of History*, p. 142.
22. Günther Bornkamm, "The Missionary Stance of Paul in I Corinthians 9 and Acts," in *Studies in Luke-Acts*, L. E. Keck and J. L. Martyn, editors (New York: Abingdon, 1966), pp. 201, 202.
23. See Paul Minear, *The Obedience of Faith: The Purpose of Paul in the Epistle to the Romans*, Studies in Biblical Theology 19 (Naperville, Ill.: Allenson, 1971), pp. 1-5.

24. See William Dyrness, "Mercy Triumphs over Justice: James 2:13 and the Theology of Faith and Works," *Themelios* 6/3 (1981):11-16.
25. *Op. cit.*, Ridderbos, *The Coming of the Kingdom*, p. 302.
26. See D. Moody Smith, "The Presentation of Jesus in the Fourth Gospel," *Interpretation* 31 (1977):393.
27. *Op. cit.*, Pannenberg, *Theology and the Kingdom of God*, p. 65.
28. See *op. cit.*, Miranda, *Marx and the Bible*, p. 88.
29. Raymond Brown, *New Testament Essays* (Garden City, N.Y.: Doubleday, 1968), p. 220.
30. See also *ibid.*, p. 228.
31. *Ibid.*, p. 241.
32. Clinton D. Morrison, "Mission and Ethic," *Interpretation* 19 (1965):265.
33. See also Paul Minear, "The Idea of Incarnation in First John," *Interpretation* 24 (1970):292-295.
34. *Ibid.*, p. 298.
35. See Alfred C. Krass, *Five Lanterns at Sundown: Evangelism in a Chastened Mood* (Grand Rapids, Mich.: Eerdmans, 1978), p. 73.
36. See *op. cit.*, Ladd, *Jesus and the Kingdom*, pp. 258-273.
37. See Carl E. Braaten, *The Flaming Center: A Theology of Christian Mission* (Philadelphia: Fortress, 1977), p. 43.
38. Ethelbert Stauffer, *New Testament Theology*, John Marsh, trans. (New York: Macmillan, 1955), p. 181.
39. *Op. cit.*, Hahn, *Mission in the New Testament*, p. 165.

14. The End and Goal of Creation: The New Heaven and New Earth

1. See Jürgen Moltmann, *A Theology of Hope*, J. W. Leitch, trans. (New York: Harper & Row, 1967), pp. 103-106.
2. See *ibid.*, p. 105.
3. See *op. cit.*, Clines, *The Theme of the Pentateuch*, pp. 69, 70.
4. N. A. Dahl, "Christ, Creation and the Church," in *op. cit.*, *The Background of the New Testament and Its Eschatology*, p. 429.
5. Elizabeth Fiorenza, "The Eschatology and Composition of the Apocalypse," *Catholic Biblical Quarterly* 30 (1968):539.
6. See Mathias Rissi, *The Future of the World: An Exegetical Study of Revelation 19:11—22:15*, Studies in Biblical Theology 23 (London: SCM, 1972), pp. 7, 8.
7. See *op. cit.*, Fiorenza, "The Eschatology and Composition of the Apocalypse," p. 562.
8. *Ibid.*
9. See G. E. Ladd, *A Commentary of the Revelation of John* (Grand Rapids, Mich.: Eerdmans, 1972), p. 99.
10. See *op. cit.*, Fiorenza, "The Eschatology and Composition of the Apocalypse," p. 566.
11. See *op. cit.*, Rissi, *The Future of the World*, p. 9.
12. John Calvin, Commentary on Matthew 28:18, 20.
13. See *op. cit.*, Berkhof, *Christ the Meaning of History*, pp. 104-106.
14. Elizabeth Fiorenza, "Redemption as Liberation: Apocalypse 1:5f and 5:9f," *Catholic Biblical Quarterly* 36 (1974):220.
15. *Op. cit.*, Mouw, *Politics and the Biblical Drama*, p. 34.
16. Michael Green, *The Second Epistle of Peter and the Epistle of Jude* (Grand Rapids, Mich.: Eerdmans, 1968), p. 138.

17. C. E. B. Cranfield, "Some Observations on Romans 8:19-21," in *op. cit.*, *Reconciliation and Hope*, R. Banks, editor, pp. 225, 226.

18. *Ibid.*, p. 228.

19. *Op. cit.*, Klein, "The Biblical Understanding of the Kingdom of God," pp. 406, 407.

20. G. R. Beasley-Murray, "How Christian Is the Book of Revelation?," in *op. cit.*, *Reconciliation and Hope*, R. Banks, editor, p. 281.

21. See *op. cit.*, Rissi, *The Future of the World*, pp. 30, 31.

22. *Ibid.*, p. 32.

23. *Op. cit.*, Beasley-Murray, "How Christian Is the Book of Revelation?," p. 281.

24. Paul Minear, "The Cosmology of the Apocalypse," in *Current Issues in New Testament Interpretation*, W. Klassen and G. G. Snyders, editors (New York: Harper, 1962), p. 36.

25. See *op. cit.*, Mouw, *Politics and the Biblical Drama*, p. 128.

26. *Op. cit.*, Miguez-Bonino, *Doing Theology in a Revolutionary Situation*, p. 152.

27. *Op. cit.*, Rissi, *The Future of the World*, p. 80.

Epilogue

1. *Op. cit.*, Jeremias, *New Testament Theology*, p. 248.

2. *Op. cit.*, W. D. Davies, *The Gospel and the Land*, p. 366.

3. *Ibid.*

4. *Op. cit.*, Miranda, *Marx and the Bible*, see pp. 36, 104, 217.

5. in *op. cit.*, Braaten, *The Flaming Center*, p. 169.

6. *Op. cit.*, Brueggemann, *The Land*, p. 186.

7. *Op. cit.*, Miranda, *Marx and the Bible*, pp. 104, 105.

8. *Op. cit.*, *Interpreter's Dictionary of the Bible, Supplementary Volume*, p. 944.

9. *Op. cit.*, Braaten, *The Flaming Center*, p. 86.

10. Richard J. Mouw, *Political Evangelism* (Grand Rapids, Mich.: Eerdmans, 1973), p. 17.

11. *Op. cit.*, Pannenberg, *Theology and the Kingdom of God*, pp. 80, 81.

12. See *op. cit.*, Berkhof, *Christ the Meaning of History*, p. 84.

13. *Op. cit.*, Braaten, *The Flaming Center*, p. 41.

14. *Op. cit.*, Berkhof, *Christ the Meaning of History*, p. 133.

15. *Ibid.*, pp. 101, 102.

16. *Op. cit.*, Blauw, *The Missionary Nature of the Church*, p. 112.

17. *Op. cit.*, Kraus, *The Healing Christ*, p. 15.

18. See *op. cit.*, Krass, *Five Lanterns at Sundown*, p. 13.

19. *Op. cit.*, Fackre, *Word in Deed*, p. 54.

20. *Op. cit.*, K. Barth, *Church Dogmatics*, IV/3, p. 874.

21. *Op. cit.*, Kraus, *The Healing Christ*, p. 47.

22. J. D. Gort, "Gospel for the Poor?," *Missiology* 7 (1979):343.

23. *Op. cit.*, Gordis, *Poets, Prophets and Sages*, p. 177.

24. *Op. cit.*, Blauw, *The Missionary Nature of the Church*, p. 105.

25. *Op. cit.*, Stott, *Christian Mission in the Modern World*, p. 30.

26. in Peter Brown, *Augustine of Hippo* (Berkeley, Calif.: University of California Press, 1967), pp. 431, 211.

27. John Bright, *The Kingdom of God* (Nashville: Abingdon, 1953), pp. 248, 249.
28. *Op. cit.*, Berkhof, *Christ the Meaning of History*, p. 91.
29. *Op. cit.*, Costas, *The Church and Its Mission*, p. 206n.
30. *Op. cit.*, K. Barth, *Church Dogmatics*, IV/1, p. 116.

Bibliography

Books

Auerbach, Erich. *Mimesis: The Representation of Reality in Western Literature*. Princeton, N. J.: Princeton University Press, 1953.

Barth, Gerhard. "Matthew's Understanding of the Law," in *Tradition and Interpretation in Matthew*, G. Bornkamm, Gerhard Barth and H. J. Held, editors, Percy Scott, trans. Philadelphia: Westminster, 1963.

Barth, Karl. "An Exegetical Study of Matthew 28:16-20," in *Theology of Christian Mission*, Gerald Anderson, editor. New York: Abingdon, 1961, pp. 55-71.

———. *Theology and Church*, E. P. Smith, trans. London: SCM, 1962.

———. *Church Dogmatics*, 13 volumes. Edinburgh: T & T Clark, 1936ff.

Baker, David. *Two Testaments: One Bible*. Downers Grove, Ill: InterVarsity Press, 1977.

Bavinck, Herman. *The Doctrine of God*. Grand Rapids, Mich.: Eerdmans, 1951.

Beasley-Murray, G. R. "How Christian Is the Book of Revelation?," in *Reconciliation and Hope*, R. Banks, editor. Grand Rapids, Mich.: Eerdmans, 1974, pp. 275-284.

Berkhof, Hendrikus. *Christ the Meaning of History*, L. Buurman, trans. London: SCM, 1966.

———. *Christian Faith: An Introduction to the Study of Faith*, S. Woudstra, trans. Grand Rapids, Mich.: Eerdmans, 1979.

Beyerhaus, Peter, *Missions: Which Way? Humanization or Redemption?* Grand Rapids, Mich.: Zondervan, 1971.

———. *Theological Foundations for Mission*. Grand Rapids, Mich.: Zondervan, 1972.

Blank, Sheldon. "Prophet as Paradigm," in *Essays in Old Testament Ethics*, J. L. Crenshaw and J. T. Willis, editors. New York: KTAV, 1974, pp. 111-130.

Blauw, Johannes. *The Missionary Nature of the Church: A Survey of the Biblical Theology of Mission*. Grand Rapids, Mich.: Eerdmans, 1962.

Bonsirven, Joseph. *Palestinian Judaism in the Time of Christ*, William Wolf, trans. New York: Holt, Rinehart and Winston, 1964.

Bornkamm, Günther. "The Missionary Stance of Paul in I Corinthians 9 and Acts," in *Studies in Luke-Acts*, L. E. Keck and J. L. Martyn, editors. New York: Abingdon, 1966, pp. 194-207.

Braaten, Carl E. *The Flaming Center: A Theology of Christian Mission*. Philadelphia: Fortress, 1977.

Bright, John. *The Kingdom of God*. Nashville: Abingdon, 1953.

_____. *Covenant and Promise: The Prophetic Understanding of the Future in Pre-exilic Israel*. Philadelphia: Westminster, 1976.

Brown, Colin, editor. *The New International Dictionary of New Testament Theology*, Volumes I-III. Grand Rapids, Mich.: Zondervan, 1976-78.

Brown, Peter. *Augustine of Hippo*. Berkeley, Calif.: University of California Press, 1967.

Brown, Raymond. *New Testament Essays*. Garden City, N.Y.: Doubleday, 1968.

Brueggemann, Walter. *Living Towards a Vision: Biblical Reflections on Shalom*. Philadelphia: United Church Press, 1976.

_____. *The Land*. Philadelphia: Fortress, 1977.

_____. *The Prophetic Imagination*. Philadelphia: Fortress, 1978.

Buttrick, George A. and Crim, Keith R., editors. *Interpreter's Dictionary of the Bible* and *Supplementary Volume*. Nashville: Abingdon, 1976.

Calvin, John. *Institutes of the Christian Religion*. Philadelphia: Westminster, 1960.

Childs, Bernard S. *Biblical Theology in Crisis*. Philadelphia: Westminster, 1970.

_____. *Introduction to the Old Testament as Scripture*. Philadelphia: Fortress, 1979.

Clines, David J. A. *The Theme of the Pentateuch*, JSOT Supplement 10. Sheffield: University of Sheffield, 1978.

Costas, Orlando E. *The Church and Its Mission: A Shattering Critique from the Third World*. Wheaton, Ill.: Tyndale House, 1974.

Cranfield, C. E. B. "Some Observations on Romans 8:19-21," in *Reconciliation and Hope*, R. Banks, editor. Grand Rapids, Mich.: Eerdmans, 1974, pp. 224-230.

Cullmann, Oscar. "Eschatology and Missions in the New Testament," in *The Background of the New Testament and Its Eschatology*, W. D. Davies and D. Daube, editors. New York: Cambridge University Press, 1964.

_____. *Christ and Time*, F. Filson, trans. Philadelphia: Westminster, 1946.

_____. *Salvation in History*. New York: Harper & Row, 1967.

Dahl, N. A. "Christ, Creation and the Church," in *The Background of the New Testament and Its Eschatology*, W. D. Davies and D. Daube, editors. New York: Cambridge University Press, 1964, pp. 422-443.

Davidson, A. B. *The Theology of the Old Testament*. Edinburgh: T & T Clark, 1904.

Davies, J. G. *Worship and Mission*. New York: Association Press, 1967.

Davies, W. D. *The Gospel and the Land: Early Christianity and Jewish Territorial Doctrine*. Berkeley, Calif.: University of California Press, 1974.

Dodd, C. H. *The Apostolic Preaching and Its Developments*. London: Hodder & Stoughton, 1944.

_____. *The Founder of Christianity*. London: Macmillan, 1970.

Douglas, J. D., editor. *New Bible Dictionary*. Grand Rapids, Mich.: Eerdmans, 1975.

Dyrness, W. A. *Themes in Old Testament Theology*. Downers Grove, Ill.: Inter-Varsity Press, 1979.

Edwards, Jonathan. *The End for Which God Created the World: Works of President Edwards*, Vol. II. New York: Leavitt & Allen, 1858.

Eichrodt, Walter. *Man in the Old Testament*, Studies in Biblical Theology 4, K. and R. Smith, trans. London: SCM, 1951.

_____. *Theology of the Old Testament*, 2 volumes, J. A. Baker, trans. Philadelphia: Westminster, 1961, 1967.

Fackre, Gabriel. *Do and Tell: Engagement Evangelism in the Seventies*. Grand Rapids, Mich.: Eerdmans, 1973.

_____. *Word in Deed: Theological Themes in Evangelism*. Grand Rapids, Mich.: Eerdmans, 1975.

Frend, W. H. L. *Martyrdom and Persecution in the Early Church*. New York: Oxford University Press, 1965.

Gordis, Robert. *Poets, Prophets and Sages: Essays in Biblical Interpretation*. Bloomington, Ind.: Indiana University Press, 1971.

Green, Michael. *The Second Epistle of Peter and the Epistle of Jude*. Grand Rapids, Mich.: Eerdmans, 1968.

Gunkel, Herman. *The Legends of Genesis: The Biblical Saga and History*. New York: Schocken Books, 1964.

Gutierrez, Gustavo. *A Theology of Liberation*. Maryknoll, N.Y.: Orbis, 1973.

Hahn, Ferdinand. *Mission in the New Testament*, Studies in Biblical Theology 47, Frank Clarke, trans. Naperville, Ill.: Allenson, 1965.

Hancock, Robert Lincoln, editor. *The Ministry of Development in Evangelical Perspective*. Pasadena, Calif.: William Carey Library, 1979.

Hengel, Martin. *Judaism and Hellenism*. Philadelphia: Fortress, 1974.

_____. *Property and Riches in the Early Church*. Philadelphia: Fortress, 1974.

Hill, David. *The Gospel of Matthew*. London: Oliphants, 1972.

Jeremias, Joachim. *Jesus' Promise to the Nations*, Studies in Biblical Theology 24. London: SCM, 1967.

_____. *New Testament Theology*, John Bowden, trans. New York: Scribner's, 1971.

_____. *The Parables of Jesus*, S. H. Hooke, trans. London: SCM, 1972.

Johnston, Arthur. *The Battle for World Evangelism*. Wheaton, Ill.: Tyndale House, 1978.

Juliana of Norwich. *Revelations of Divine Love*. New York: Doubleday, 1977.

Kaiser, Walter, Jr. *Toward an Old Testament Theology*. Grand Rapids, Mich.: Zondervan, 1978.

Kidner, Derek. *Proverbs*. London: Tyndale, 1964.

Kittel, G. and Friedrich, G., editors. *Theological Dictionary of the New Testament*, 10 volumes. Grand Rapids, Mich.: Eerdmans, 1964ff.

Krass, Alfred C. *Five Lanterns at Sundown: Evangelism in a Chastened Mood*. Grand Rapids, Mich.: Eerdmans, 1978.

Kraus, C. Norman. *The Healing Christ*. Scottdale, Pa.: Herald, 1972.

Kümmel, W. G. *Theology of the New Testament*, J. D. Steely, trans. London: SCM, 1974.

Ladd, G. E. *Jesus and the Kingdom*. New York: Harper & Row, 1964.

_____. *A Commentary on the Revelation of John*. Grand Rapids, Mich.: Eerdmans, 1972.

_____. "Apocalyptic and New Testament Theology," in *Reconciliation and Hope*, R. Banks, editor. Grand Rapids, Mich.: Eerdmans, 1974, pp. 285-296.

Lohse, Eduard. *The New Testament Environment*, J. S. Steely, trans. Nashville: Abingdon, 1976.

Longenecker, R. N. *Paul the Apostle of Liberty*. Grand Rapids, Mich.: Baker, 1976.

Marshall, I. H. *Luke: Historian and Theologian*. Grand Rapids, Mich.: Zondervan, 1971.

———. *The Gospel of Luke*. Grand Rapids, Mich.: Eerdmans, 1978.

———. *Acts: An Introduction and Commentary*. Leicester: Inter-Varsity Press, 1980.

Miguez-Bonino, Jose. *Doing Theology in a Revolutionary Situation*. Philadelphia: Fortress, 1975.

Minear, Paul. *And Great Shall Be Your Reward*. New Haven, Conn.: Yale University Press, 1942.

———. "The Cosmology of the Apocalypse," in *Current Issues in New Testament Interpretation*, W. Klassen and G. G. Snyders, editors. New York: Harper, 1962, pp. 23-37.

———. *The Obedience of Faith: The Purpose of Paul in the Epistle to the Romans*, Studies in Biblical Theology 19. Naperville, Ill.: Allenson, 1971.

———. *To Heal and to Reveal: Prophetic Vocation According to Luke*. New York: Seabury, 1976.

Milton, John. *Paradise Lost*. New York: New American Library, 1961.

Miranda, Jose. *Marx and the Bible: A Critique of the Philosophy of Oppression*. Maryknoll, N.Y.: Orbis, 1974.

Moltmann, Jürgen. *A Theology of Hope*, J. W. Leitch, trans. New York: Harper & Row, 1967.

Mouw, Richard. *Political Evangelism*. Grand Rapids, Mich.: Eerdmans, 1973.

———. *Politics and the Biblical Drama*. Grand Rapids, Mich.: Eerdmans, 1976.

Newbigins, Lesslie. *The Open Secret*. Grand Rapids, Mich.: Eerdmans, 1978.

Nickle, Keith F. *The Collection: A Study in Paul's Strategy*, Studies in Biblical Theology 48. London: SCM, 1966.

Pannenberg, Wolfhart. *Theology and the Kingdom of God*, R. J. Neuhaus, editor. Philadelphia: Westminster, 1969.

Ridderbos, Herman. *The Coming of the Kingdom*. Philadelphia: Presbyterian and Reformed, 1962.

———. *Paul: An Outline of His Theology*, J. R. Dewitt, trans. Grand Rapids, Mich.: Eerdmans, 1975.

Rissi, Mathias. *The Future of the World: An Exegetical Study of Revelation 19:11—22:15*, Studies in Biblical Theology 23. London: SCM, 1972.

Rottenberg, Isaac C. *The Promise and the Presence: Toward a Theology of the Kingdom of God*. Grand Rapids, Mich.: Eerdmans, 1980.

Rowley, H. H. *The Missionary Message of the Old Testament*. London: Carey Press, 1944.

Scott, Waldron. *Bring Forth Justice: A Contemporary Perspective on Mission*. Grand Rapids, Mich.: Eerdmans, 1980.

Shepherd, Norman. "The Covenant Context for Evangelism," in *The New Testament Student and Theology*, John Skilton, editor. Philadelphia: Presbyterian and Reformed, 1976.

Sider, Ronald J. *Rich Christians in an Age of Hunger*. Downers Grove, Ill.: InterVarsity Press, 1977.

———, editor. *Evangelicals and Development*. London: Marshall Morgan and Scott, 1981.

Stauffer, Ethelbert. *New Testament Theology*, John Marsh, trans. New York: Macmillan, 1955.

Stott, John R. W. *Christian Mission in the Modern World*. Downers Grove, Ill.: InterVarsity Press, 1975.

Taylor, Vincent. *The Gospel According to St. Mark*. London: Macmillan, 1966.

Theissen, Gerd. *Sociology of Early Palestinian Christianity*, John Bowden, trans. Philadelphia: Fortress, 1978.

Tolkien, J. R. R. "On Fairy-stories," *Essays Presented to Charles Williams*, C. S. Lewis, editor. New York: Oxford University Press, 1947.

Underhill, Evelyn. *Lent*. G. P. Mellick Belshaw, editor. London: Mowbray, 1964.

van Ruler, Arnold A. *The Christian Church and the Old Testament*, G. W. Bromiley, trans. Grand Rapids, Mich.: Eerdmans, 1971.

Verkuyl, J. *Contemporary Missiology*, Dale Cooper, trans. Grand Rapids, Mich.: Eerdmans, 1978.

von Rad, Gerhard. *Genesis,* John Mark, trans. Philadelphia: Westminster, 1961.
_____. *Old Testament Theology*, 2 volumes, D. M. G. Stalker, trans. New York: Harper & Row, 1962, 1965.

Vos, Geerhardus. *Pauline Eschatology*. Grand Rapids, Mich.: Eerdmans, 1952.

Vriezen, T. C. "Essentials of the Theology of Isaiah," in *Israel's Prophetic Heritage*, B. W. Anderson and W. Harrelson, editors. London: SCM, 1962, pp. 128-146.

Wenham, John W. *The Goodness of God*. Downers Grove, Ill.: InterVarsity Press, 1974.

Westermann, Claus. *A Thousand Years and a Day*. Philadelphia: Muhlenberg, 1962.
_____. *Creation*, John J. Scullion, trans. London: Society for Propagation of Christian Knowledge, 1974.

Wilder, A. N. "Kerygma, Eschatology and Social Ethics," in *The Background of the New Testament and Its Eschatology*, W. D. Davies and D. Daube, editors. New York: Cambridge University Press, 1964, pp. 509-536.

Wolff, H. W. *Anthropology of the Old Testament*, M. Kohl, trans. Philadelphia: Fortress, 1974.

Yoder, John Howard. *The Politics of Jesus*. Grand Rapids, Mich.: Eerdmans, 1972.

Your Kingdom Come: Mission Perspectives and Reports on World Conference on Mission and Evangelism, Melbourne. Geneva: World Council of Churches.

Periodicals

Achtemeier, Paul J., "Mark as Interpreter of the Jesus Tradition," *Interpretation* 32 (1978):339-352.

Albright, William F., "From the Patriarchs to Moses," *The Biblical Archaeologist* 36 (1973):5-33, 48-76.

Brueggemann, Walter, "David and His Theologian," *Catholic Biblical Quarterly* 30 (1968):156-181.

Campbell, E. F., Jr., "Moses and the Foundation of Israel," *Interpretation* 29 (1975):141-154.

Childs, Bernard S., "The Canonical Shape of the Prophetic Literature," *Interpretation* 32 (1978):46-55.

Davies, G. Henton, "The Clues of the Kingdom in the Bible," *Interpretation* 14 (1960):155-160.

Donahue, John R., "Jesus as the Parable of God in the Gospel of Mark," *Interpretation* 32 (1978):369-386.

Dyrness, W. A., "Mercy Triumphs over Justice: James 2:13 and the Theology of Faith and Works," *Themelios* 6/3 (1981):11-16.

Eichrodt, Walter, "The Holy One in Your Midst: The Theology of Hosea," *Interpretation* 15 (1961):259-273.

Fiorenza, Elizabeth, "The Eschatology and Composition of the Apocalypse," *Catholic Biblical Quarterly* 30 (1968):537-569.

———, "Redemption as Liberation: Apocalypse 1:5f and 5:9f," *Catholic Biblical Quarterly* 36 (1974):220-232.

Freedman, David Noel, " 'Son of Man, Can These Bones Live?': The Exile," *Interpretation* 29 (1975):171-186.

Gort, J. D., "Gospel for the Poor?", *Missiology* 7 (1979):325-354.

Gunn, David M., "David and the Gift of the Kingdom," *Semeia* 3 (1975):14-15.

Hanson, Paul D., "Old Testament Apocalyptic Reconsidered," *Interpretation* 25 (1971):454-479.

Harrelson, Walter, "Guidance in the Wilderness," *Interpretation* 13 (1959):24-36.

Huffmon, Herbert B., "The Treaty Background of the Hebrew YADA," *Bulletin of American School of Oriental Research* 181 (1966):31-37; 184:36-38.

Kingsbury, Jack Dean, "The Structure of Matthew's Gospel and His Concept of Salvation-history," *Catholic Biblical Quarterly* 35 (1973):451-474.

Klein, Gunter, "The Biblical Understanding of the Kingdom of God," *Interpretation* 26 (1970):387-418.

McCarthy, Dennis J., "II Samuel and the Structure of Deuteronomic History," *Journal of Biblical Literature* 84 (1965):131-138.

———, "The Inauguration of Monarchy in Israel: A Form Critical Study of I Samuel 8—12," *Interpretation* 27 (1973):401-412.

Mendenhall, George E., "The Monarchy," *Interpretation* 29 (1975):155-170.

Mihelic, Joseph L., "Dialogue with God: A Study of Some of Jeremiah's Confessions," *Interpretation* 14 (1960):43-50.

Miller, Patrick, Jr., "The Gift of God: The Deuteronomic Theology of the Land," *Interpretation* 23 (1969):451-465.

———, "The Blessing of God," *Interpretation* 29 (1975):240-251.

Minear, Paul, "The Idea of Incarnation in First John," *Interpretation* 24 (1970):291-302.

Morrison, Clinton D., "Mission and Ethic," *Interpretation* 19 (1965):259-273.

Muilenberg, James, "Abraham and the Nations," *Interpretation* 19 (1965):387-398.

North, C. R., "The Redeemer God," *Interpretation* 2 (1948):3-16.

Parker, Thomas D., "The Political Meaning of the Doctrine of the Trinity," *Journal of Religion* 60 (1980):165-184.

Sanders, James A., "Torah and Christ," *Interpretation* 29 (1975):372-390.

Smith, D. Moody, "The Presentation of Jesus in the Fourth Gospel," *Interpretation* 31 (1977):367-378.

Talmon, Shemaryahu, "The Biblical Concept of Jerusalem," *Journal of Ecumenical Studies* 8 (1971):300-316.

Taylor, Arch B., Jr., "Decision in the Desert: The Temptation of Jesus in the Light of Deuteronomy," *Interpretation* 14 (1960):300-309.

von Rad, Gerhard, "Ancient Word and Living Word," *Interpretation* 15 (1961):3-13.

Westermann, Claus, "God and His People: The Church in the Old Testament," *Interpretation* 17 (1963):259-270.

————, "The Role of Lament in the Theology of the Old Testament," *Interpretation* 28 (1974):20-38.

Wharton, James A., "The Secret of Y," *Interpretation* 27 (1973):48-66.

Wolff, H. W., "Masters and Slaves," *Interpretation* 27 (1973):259-272.

Zimmerli, Walter, "The Message of the Prophet Ezekiel," *Interpretation* 23 (1969):131-157.